ST. PETERSBURG

PORTRAIT OF AN IMPERIAL CITY

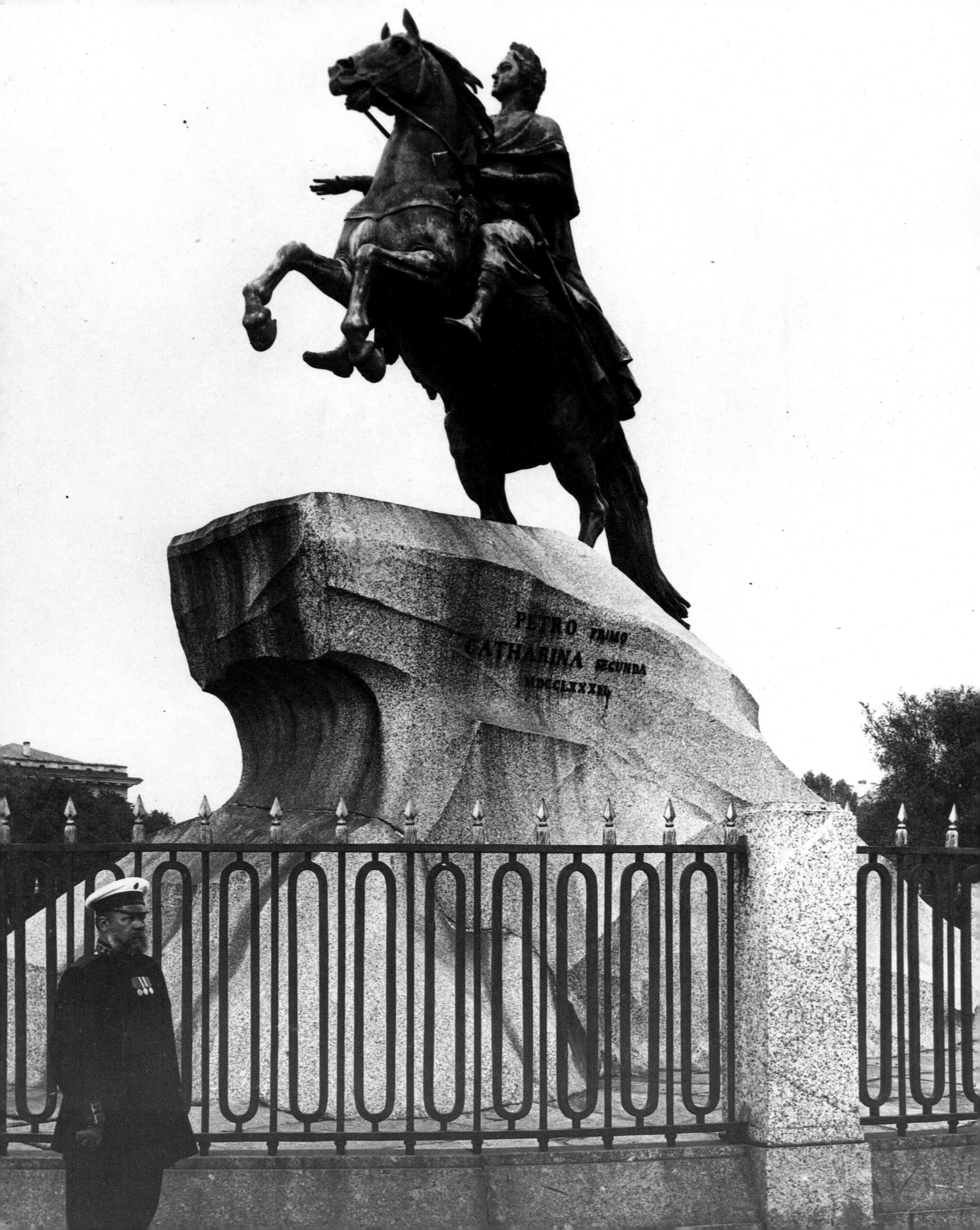
PETRO PRIMO
CATHARINA SECUNDA
MDCCLXXXII

ST. PETERSBURG

PORTRAIT OF AN IMPERIAL CITY

BORIS OMETEV AND JOHN STUART
COMPILED BY OLGA SUSLOVA AND LILY UKHTOMSKAYA

The Vendome Press

Frontispiece: This most famous monument to Peter was erected by Catherine the Great, who saw herself as heir and promoter of the Petrine inheritance, hence the concise inscription on the plinth: To Peter I from Catherine II. The statue was the work of the Frenchman, Falconet (1716–91), the head being cast separately by his student, Marie Collot, when she was only nineteen. The base of the sculpture is a gigantic boulder, dragged all the way from the shores of the Gulf of Finland and on which, so it was said, Peter had once stood. The monument was unveiled on 7 August 1782, the centenary of Peter's accession. On a rearing horse which crushes the serpent of sedition beneath its hooves, Peter, with stern expression, his hand raised to point towards the West, seems to breathe life into the city which was his creation and of which this monument is the vital symbol, a significance which is made explicit in Pushkin's celebrated poem, *The Bronze Horseman.*

Picture credits
We are grateful to the following sources for allowing us to reproduce the pictures on the pages listed:
Mary Evans Picture Library, 43
Monsieur Jacques Ferrand, 57 (bottom), 101 (top), 111, 118, 128, 197
Sotheby's, London, 94 (top right), 95 (top right), 97 (right), 98–9, 100, 101 (bottom), 102, 103, 106–7, 108, 110 (bottom), 112 (top), 113 (bottom), 116–17, 127 (top)
John Massey Stewart, 55 (top)

All other pictures were drawn from archives in the USSR.

Published in the USA in 1990 by the Vendome Press,
515, Madison Avenue, New York City, NY 1022

Distributed in the USA by Rizzoli International Publications Inc,
300 Park Avenue South, New York, NY 10010

Library of Congress Cataloging-in-Publication Data
Ometev, Boris.
  St. Petersburg.

  1. Leningrad (R.S.F.S.R.) - - Civilisation.
2. Leningrad (R.S.F.S.R.) - - History. I. Stuart, John.
II. Title. III. Title: Saint Petersburg.
DK557.044 1990   947′.453   90–12220
ISBN 0–86565–120–5

This book was designed and produced by
John Calmann and King Ltd, London

Designed by Karen Stafford
Typeset by Fakenham Photosetting Ltd, Fakenham, Norfolk
Printed in Italy by Graphicom SRL

Contents

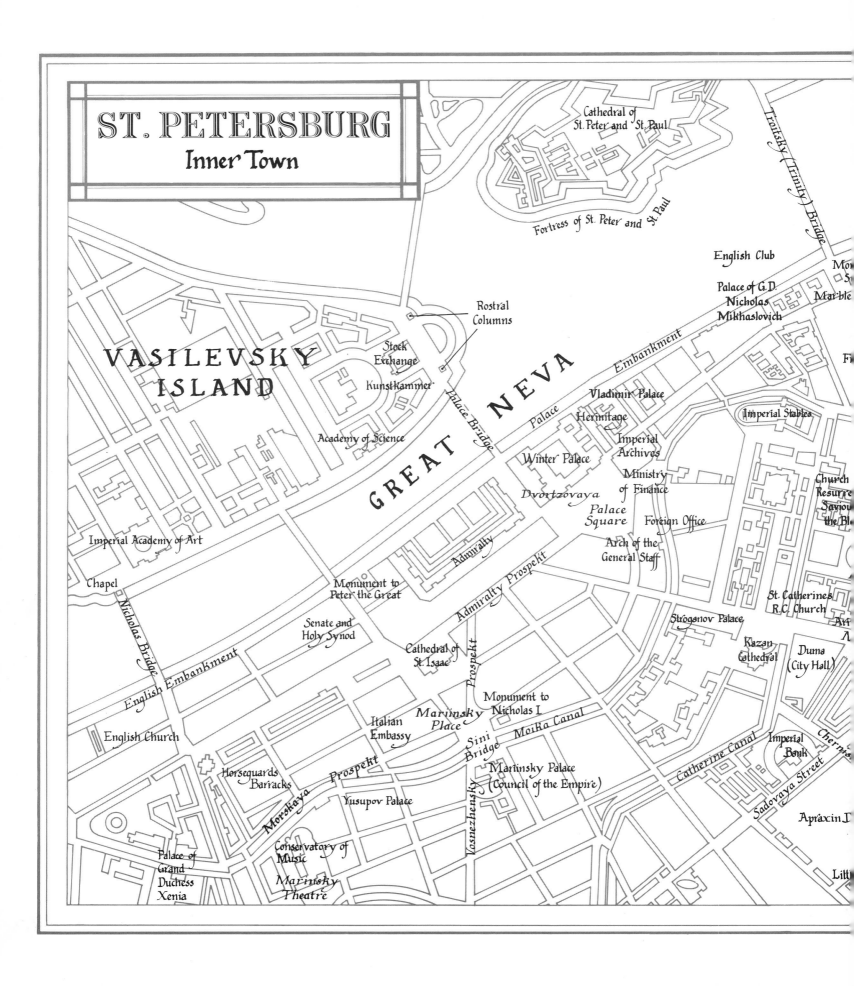

ST. PETERSBURG
Inner Town

Cathedral of
St. Peter and St. Paul

Fortress of St. Peter and St. Paul

Troitsky (Trinity) Bridge

English Club

Palace of G.D.
Nicholas
Mikhaslovich

Mar'ble

Rostral
Columns

Stock
Exchange

KunstKammer

VASILEVSKY
ISLAND

Academy of Science

Palace

Embankment

GREAT NEVA

Vladimir Palace

Hermitage

Imperial Stables

Imperial
Archives

Winter Palace

Church
Resurre
Saviou
the Bl

Dvortzovaya

Ministry
of Finance

Imperial Academy of Art

Palace
Square

Foreign Office

Chapel

Admiralty

Arch of the
General Staff

St. Catherines
R.C. Church

Monument to
Peter the Great

Admiralty Prospekt

Strogonov Palace

Kazan
Cathedral

Duma
(City Hall)

Nicholas Bridge

Senate and
Holy Synod

Prospekt

Cathedral of
St. Isaac

English Embankment

Monument to
Nicholas I

Mariinsky
Place

Sini
Bridge

Moika Canal

English Church

Italian
Embassy

Catherine Canal

Imperial
Bank

Chern

Vosnezhensky

Mariinsky Palace
(Council of the Empire)

Sadovaya Street

Horseguards
Barracks

Morskaya

Prospekt

Yusupov Palace

Apraxin D

Palace of
Grand
Duchess
Xenia

Conservatory of
Music

Mariinsky
Theatre

Litt

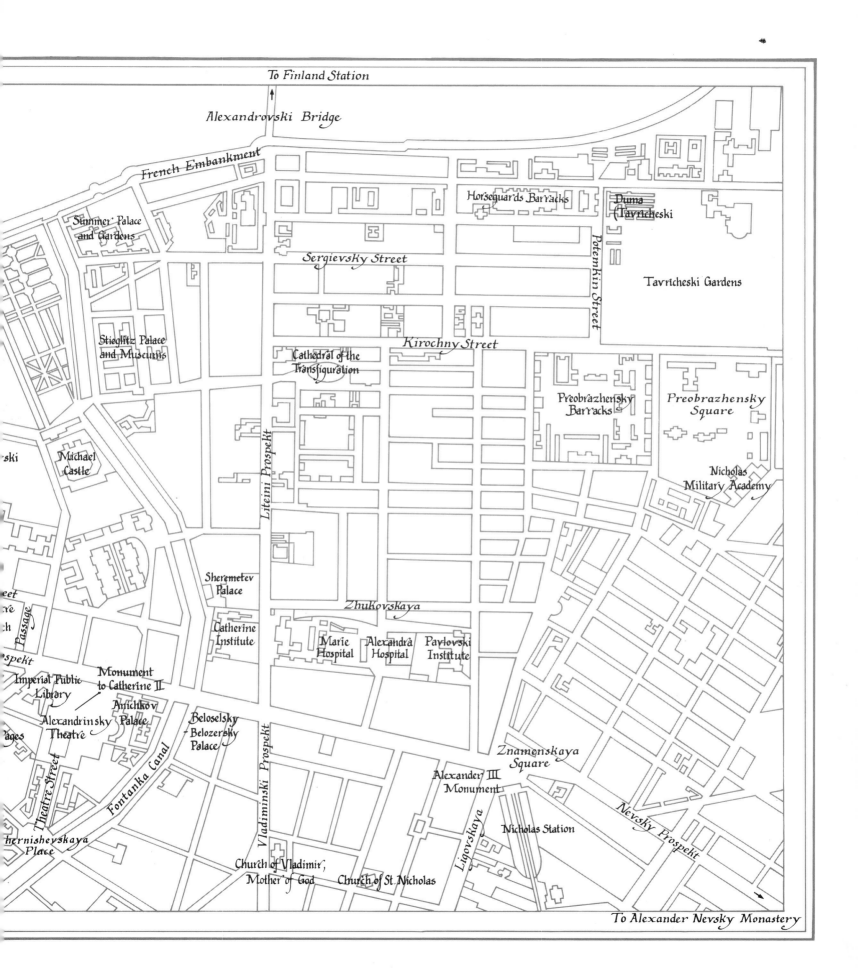

To Finland Station

Alexandrovski Bridge

French Embankment

Summer Palace and Gardens

Horseguards Barracks

Duma (Tavricheski)

Sergievsky Street

Tavricheski Gardens

Stieglitz Palace and Museums

Kirochny Street

Cathedral of the Transfiguration

Preobrazhensky Barracks

Preobrazhensky Square

Michael Castle

Nicholas Military Academy

Liteini Prospekt

Sheremetev Palace

Zhukovskaya

Catherine Institute

Marie Hospital

Alexandra Hospital

Pavlovski Institute

Imperial Public Library

Monument to Catherine II

Anichkov Palace

Alexandrinsky Theatre

Beloselsky-Belozersky Palace

Passage

Theatre Street

Fontanka Canal

Vladiminski Prospekt

Znamenskaya Square

Alexander III Monument

Chernishevskaya Place

Ligovskaya

Nicholas Station

Nevsky Prospekt

Church of Vladimir, Mother of God

Church of St. Nicholas

Potemkin Street

To Alexander Nevsky Monastery

INTRODUCTION

The grandiose Imperial capital of St. Petersburg arose on the delta of the great Neva River, spreading along a network of granite-lined canals. The city – the Venice of the North – was designed to serve, in the words of Pushkin, as 'a window on the West'. From its inauguration in 1703 until the collapse of the Empire in 1917, Petersburg provides an essential key for an understanding of the lifestyle and climate of ideas of Peter's westernised Empire. Peter the Great was the grand architect of the period, and was acclaimed during his lifetime as 'the Father of the Fatherland', without regard to his august predecessors, St. Vladimir or Ivan the Great. His city, whose name commemorates in a foreign tongue that of its creator, was built at enormous cost to human life on a remote, marshy wasteland that Peter had earlier wrested from Sweden. Seizing a bayonet from one of his soldiers, Peter is said to have dug out a piece of turf, proclaiming, 'Here a city will arise!'

Successive autocrats, the arbiters of taste, whose patronage of the arts was an essential aspect of their Imperial role, left their mark on the city through a choice of architects whose work matched their vision. It is necessary to recall them, their aspirations, and the impetus and development of art during their reigns in order to understand the shape and nature of the city at the time these photographs were taken.

For Peter, the founding of St. Petersburg served on the one hand the practical purpose of providing an essential port, accessible throughout the year, the first in Russia that was not immobilised during the winter months; on the other hand, it was a symbolic act, not unlike the founding of Constantinople. It must be remembered that Peter anticipated the Bolsheviks in his detestation of the indigenous culture, which he wished to replace with Western secular 'enlightenment'. His adoption of the title of 'Emperor' in place of 'Tsar' signalled Russia's transformation from a theocratic Orthodox state into an absolute monarchy on the lines of the most advanced Western nations. In moving the seat of government and the court to his new capital, Peter compelled three hundred of the great aristocratic families of Russia to move there also, thus weakening the power base of the nobility in Moscow. In the cultural sphere, art in the new capital, losing its religious connotations, was to come to reflect the aesthetics and taste of Western Europe.

Ruthless, cruel, and prepared to do violence to the most cherished traditions of his subjects, Peter was above all a technocrat. Art and culture failed to claim his interest because he lacked a reflective turn of mind, the spiritual dimension necessary for its appreciation. He liked seascapes, scale models, *trompe l'oeil*, and the odd pornographic picture concealed on the reverse of shutters. He was fascinated by freaks of nature. He preserved two-headed kittens and other natural curiosities. When the first museum in Petersburg, the *Kunstkammer*, was opened, his method of encouraging his countrymen towards self-education was to institute a refreshment room where giants, dwarfs and monsters were recruited to serve visitors with vodka or coffee. A utilitarian, he was primarily concerned with practical knowledge – surgery, shipbuilding, the construction of a fort or the circulation of a fish. His stay in Holland, where he had learned the art of shipbuilding, made a strong impression on him, and the houses of his new capital were simple, stuccoed wooden and brick cabins, based on the Dutch model and painted to look like stone. Almost all trace of this part of Peter's city has disappeared, although the original cabin he built for himself and his modest Dutch pavilion in the Summer Garden survive.

The Cathedral of St. Peter and St. Paul, in the fortress of the same name constructed by Peter on an island in the Neva, was, as Hamilton, the noted historian of Russian art, aptly puts it, 'to assume a venerated position in the legend of St. Petersburg as an Imperial city'. The architect was Tressini, discovered by Peter's ambassador working in Copenhagen; he was an interpreter of the Northern Baroque style which owed much to Holland. As a reflection of Peter's protestant inclinations, the Cathedral was the first structure in Russia where the emphasis on the traditional dome was replaced by a spire. This needle-like spire, rising above the tombs of Peter and his successors, became an essential feature of the city's skyline, and struck a note echoed by the masts of the countless ships which came to fill the river, bringing to the waterfront 'a mingled fragrance of unfamiliar spices, oranges, lemons, vanilla and tar', as E. M. Almedingen remembers.

But it is the monument to Peter erected by Catherine II which is the true symbol of the city, evoking the terrifying presence of this ruthless giant, determined to alter the course of history. His rearing horse tramples the serpent of sedition beneath its hooves, his fierce gaze pierces the passer-by, and his right hand is raised triumphantly towards the West.

The great schism in Russian life, which was already fragmented after the crisis of a church schism in the seventeenth century, originated with Peter. He had a protestant disposition, and his so-called church reform in fact amounted to the subjugation of the church to the state on a protestant model. Peter's ecclesiastical 'reform' – the abolition of the Patriarchate and its replacement by a Ministry of Religious Affairs – was the keystone of his revolution. In 1699, the Bishop of Salisbury, recording a four-hour conversation he had had with Peter, noted his serious concern with ecclesiastical affairs: 'He harkened to no part of what I told him than when I explained the authority . . . the supremacy of our kings . . . I insisted much to show him the great designs of Christianity in the reforming men's hearts and minds, which he assured me he would apply himself to.' The Petrine state absorbed everything within its authority, and after Peter the Russian people existed on two levels – a Westernised upper level of society, who were estranged from the native traditions of the people, and the masses, who remained for the most part unaffected by his changes. The full consequences of this split were to become apparent only later. In Petersburg, an alien city built by Western architects, the drama of the Westernisation of Russia's destiny was played out.

In 1741, when a coup brought Peter's daughter Elizabeth to the throne, a foreign observer described the architecture of Peter's city as displaying a mixture of Italian, French and Dutch influences, with the latter predominant. Elizabeth, however, had once toyed with the idea of marrying Louis XV, and her natural predilection was for the scintillating splendour of the French court. Of a frivolous disposition and with an insatiable taste for entertainment and masquerade, she was nevertheless kind-hearted, and her reign saw a renewal of cultural life after the savage pragmatism of Peter. It was she who founded the Imperial Porcelain Factory, the Academy of Art and the Imperial Theatres in St. Petersburg. Architecture was the most vital art form in Russia during the eighteenth and early nineteenth centuries. Throughout the twenty years of Elizabeth's reign, her vision was realised through the work of Count Bartolomeo Rastrelli, the son of an Italian sculptor, who had come to Russia at the age of fifteen. As court architect, Rastrelli built a number of graceful buildings in the current rococo style, among them the Smolny Convent, the Summer and Winter Palaces, and town houses for the Stroganov and Varontsov families. With their primary colours, curvilinear outlines and gesticulating figures on the rooftops, these buildings epitomise the theatrical tastes of Russia's Elizabethan age.

As a legacy of this era there is one building which perhaps more than any other evokes the city's life force – the Winter Palace, built between 1754 and 1762. The scene of epoch-making events, it provided for over two hundred years the setting for the apotheosis of the monarchy, and was constantly embellished and refurbished by outstanding architect-designers, cabinet-makers, silversmiths and other craftsmen. Superbly sited on the river bank at the heart of the city, the Palace complex was the theatrical *mise-en-scène* – the citizens of Petersburg became familiar with its courtyard, gateways and the lit windows of its vast, broken façade as the backdrop to an unending spectacle of Imperial public appearances, military parades and the habitual comings and goings of ministers and foreign plenipotentiaries in carriages emblazoned with the Imperial arms. Everyday events were interwoven with pageantry in such a way that the most ordinary mechanics of government were interwoven with the majesty of Imperial power.

There were also the religious ceremonies held in the city. Among the most noteworthy of these was the blessing of the River Neva in front of the Winter Palace, a ceremony of renewal and resanctification which took place at Epiphany, 6 January. While the ladies of the court passed through the enfilade of formal halls to watch from the windows, the troops stood below in the freezing cold at the water's edge. A hole was cut in the ice beneath a canopy of gold brocade. The Metropolitan's gold cross was dipped three times into 'the Jordan', while the Emperor, his head bared, stood among his soldiers in the sub-zero winter temperature.

The focus for the most important religious ceremonies of the city was to be concentrated in the three monumental structures which dominated its skyline – the Alexander Nevsky monastery, the Kazan Cathedral and the Church of St. Isaac. The first was founded in the reign of Peter, who, to placate the people by adding an auspicious spiritual dimension to his new capital, had brought here the relics of St. Alexander of the Neva, the great thirteenth-century defender of the Russian land who had defeated the Swedes and the Teutonic knights and had thereby ensured the survival of Russian culture. This was the main monastic establishment of St. Petersburg, founded by a man who had shown himself strongly antagonistic to monasticism.

The Cathedral of the Kazan Virgin, built between 1801 and 1811, enshrined one of the three miracle-working prototypes of the virgin, a protective talisman – a palladium of the city. The cathedral was to be intimately linked with many aspects of the life of Petersburg. Here monarchs came to pray when they went to war, and here prayers were offered for deceased Emperors before their mortal remains were taken in procession to the Peter Paul Fortress. It is curious that despite the insistence that its structure should be entirely Russian and that to this end the commission was entrusted to the gifted architect Voronikhin, it could hardly look more Roman; its semi-circular colonnade was in fact inspired by St. Peter's in Rome. The church interior houses military banners captured from the French invaders during the Napoleonic war and many embellishments made from tons of silver recovered by Cossacks from the retreating French and presented by them to the Kazan Virgin.

9

But it is the massive silhouette of St. Isaac's, completed in 1858, which, more than any other, dominates the city. Its vast interior, sumptuously ornamented with lapis and malachite, was filled with expectant crowds on the great feast days, and for those who attended the service on Easter night the experience was unforgettable. Outside, flames rose from the bronze torches held by angels at the four corners of the roof, and the noise of the Cathedral's bells reverberated across the square. Within, tens of thousands of unlit candles, linked by a thread of gun cotton, outlined the vaults of the architecture. When Christ's resurrection was re-enacted, a flame passed along the thread, igniting each candle with immense dramatic effect, while the packed crowd below also passed on the light to each other's candles, and the beautiful melodies of the Russian Easter hymn were heard against the ringing of church bells all over the city.

After the brief reign of Elizabeth's successor, Peter, it was the latter's consort, Catherine the Great, who indelibly marked the city with her vision translated into stone. Her artistic tastes were totally opposed to those of Elizabeth. If Peter the Great could be called 'the crowned Bolshevik', Catherine was the reigning intellectual. She found the endless masquerades and frivolity of the Elizabethan age an embarrassment – significantly, while Elizabeth's favourite colours had been pink with a profusion of gold, Catherine preferred much more subdued ranges of blue and violet, opaline glass and bronze. Of herself she wrote, 'I am every inch the gentleman with a mind much more male than female. But together with this I [am] anything but masculine and combine with the mind and temperament of a man the attractions of a lovable woman.' She rose early and lit her own fire before setting herself to work and enjoyed intelligent conversation with her inner circle, who were encouraged to dispense with formality. As a German who had usurped the throne, she was clever enough to know how to ingratiate herself with her subjects, particularly by appearing deferential to the religious tradition of the country which her husband had held in visible contempt. Her untiring patronage of the arts brought immense prestige to the Empire. Her proposed legal code, with its advanced principles borrowed from the latest Western philosophical treatises, was seen by Voltaire as winning for her more glory than 'ten victories on the Danube'. But there was always something cold and unfathomable about her which did not escape even those who admired her.

Catherine ordered the construction of the Hermitage in a subdued classical style which contrasts sharply with the effervescent Winter Palace, to which it is connected. Catherine liked to withdraw here with a few chosen companions, and here she hung her collection of European paintings. She was the first Russian sovereign to develop a discriminating eye for European painting; her grandson, Alexander I, was still unpacking boxes of her acquisitions a generation after her death.

Catherine was fortunate in securing the services of a French architect working in Petersburg, Vallin de la Mothe, to whom she entrusted the construction of the original Hermitage and the Imperial Academy. Another talented architect, the Italian Antonio Rinaldi built the Marble Palace as a gift for Catherine's favourite, Grigorii Orlov. The German architect Velten was responsible for the construction of the severe and dignified quays which line the network of canals on the riverfront. However, the two names which figure most prominently during her reign are those of a Scot and an Italian, Cameron and Quarenghi.

Charles Cameron, whom Catherine described in a letter as 'a Jacobite by profession', was appreciated by the Empress as an expert on Palladio who had written a treatise on Roman baths. He designed the austerely beautiful gallery at Tsarskoye Selo which contrasts strongly with the playful Elizabethan rococo adjoining it. Quarenghi, who worked in Russia for nearly forty years, was a gifted exponent of a classical and Palladian style. His work is simple, powerful and serene, and if Cameron is noted for his small-scale palaces and pleasure pavilions in landscaped parks, Quarenghi excelled in the design of magnificent public buildings; the State Bank, the Academy of Sciences, the Women's Institute, the Hermitage Theatre and – perhaps his masterpiece – the graceful Alexander Palace are all his work.

Paul, the son of Catherine and Peter III, was thrust into the background during his mother's reign. A tragic and complex figure, he lived in isolation at his court at Pavlovsk and later at Gatchina. His antipathy for his mother led him to dislike everything she stood for, but his own taste, and especially that of his wife, the gifted Maria Feodorovna, was outstanding. Together they made a celebrated journey to Western Europe under the pseudonyms of the Comte and Comtesse du Nord, returning laden with presents and acquisitions. So much in Paul's life was failure that it is good to realise that his marriage at least was a happy and fulfilling one. The interior furnishings at the palace at Pavlovsk exemplify the taste of Maria, and they have survived intact to our time. She left an inventory explaining where each piece of furniture should stand, and a number of intaglios and hardstone carvings that are the work of her hand still survive. The mother of three successive Emperors, she lived to a great age and is remembered not solely as a patron of art and artists but also for her good works. The third notable residence built by Paul during his short reign – after the palaces of Gatchina and Pavlovsk on the city outskirts – was the sombre Michael Castle which, with its moat and its evocation of a seclusion belonging to an earlier age, reflects the suspicious and disturbed mind of its creator. At the entrance of its imposing red structure Paul caused another monument to be set up to Peter, and mindful of his mother's tribute on the plinth of the Bronze Horseman, he had this inscribed, 'To the grandfather, from the grandson'.

Paul was murdered in the Michael Castle in 1801 in a palace coup engineered by disaffected nobles. The Russian people, compassionate and appreciative of the redemptive value of suffering, always sympathised with Paul, and more candles were placed on his tomb in the Peter and Paul Fortress than on any other.

Under Catherine, Russian art and artists came of age, and she was the first Russian monarch to give commissions to native Russian architects, the most notable among them Stasov and Bajhenov. Under her hand, St. Petersburg became one of the most beautiful cities in Europe, an extraordinarily unified ensemble of predominantly neo-classical architecture. Because of the vast Russian horizons the preference of the country's people had always been for small, intimate architecture, but in Petersburg the scale was of another order – wide streets, squares designed for parades, and a broad river. Here the last great monuments of neo-classicism produced an unforgettable impression under the pale sky of a northern summer, or with the winter light playing on the coloured buildings under snow.

The accession of Catherine's favourite grandson, Alexander, gave new direction to artistic taste in the capital. Broadminded, intelligent and charming, Alexander appeared to his contemporaries as a young Apollo. His taste and energy further developed and refined the city. A passionate builder, he personally supervised plans for the new buildings in the capital with the help of the first permanent government planning commission in Europe. His taste is epitomised in the Alexandrian Empire style, a Russian version which assimilated the trends emanating from France while it retained the aristocratic flavour which had characterised European culture before the French Revolution. Victorious over Napoleon, Alexander led his armies to Paris, where he was received with rapture by the French and where the Parisians heard the alien melodies of the Russian Orthodox memorial for the dead recited for Louis XVI in the Place de la Concorde. This encounter between the Russian educated classes and Paris profoundly affected Russian ideas and aspirations, and, in the atmosphere of romantic dreams then prevalent, was to be an important factor in the abortive Decembrist revolt of 1825.

Alexander desired to make Petersburg a city without equal. His chosen architect was the Italian, Rossi, who erected a number of imposing public buildings in an Imperial 'Roman' style, intended to 'surpass that which the Romans considered sufficient for their monuments'. The Michael Palace, built for Alexander's younger brother, Grand Duke Michael, is one of the greatest manifestations of the style, conceived as part of an architectural whole, incorporating the square before it and the vast parade ground in its rear. In the same way, Theatre Street is an architectural complex of imposing beauty. There is always a sense of Imperial scale, but the scale nonetheless remains a human one.

The architecture of Alexander and that of his brother and successor Nicholas I constitute the official style up until the latter's death in 1855. Thus classicism and neo-classicism reign supreme for a period of a hundred years.

Nicholas I was a figure of heroic stature, handsome and imposing, without the easygoing demeanour of his elder brother. In time, the pressure of his role spoiled his good looks,

and he was referred to as 'Apollo with toothache'. His accession, following the mysterious death of his brother in 1825, was marred by the insurrection of a group of Guards officers, who had absorbed some philosophical ideals emanating from the West. They had no agreed programme to impose – some had aspirations for Russia to become a constitutional monarchy on the English model, others were extremists and many were anarchists. Nicholas's elder brother Constantine, who had renounced his claim to the throne and contracted a morganatic marriage, was the unwitting and unwilling figurehead for the movement.

Nicholas was the last great monarch-builder of Petersburg. Under his reign, the last coherent architectural complexes were completed. Despite the continued predominance of the neo-classic order, he also flirted with eclecticism. The strong German influence in the city and the close dynastic ties with Prussia also explain Nicholas's brief affair with Gothic. But his reign also saw the first stirrings of the controversy between Slavophiles and Westernisers, and although Nicholas did not participate directly in either camp, he did show an interest in the resurgence of old Russian stylistic motifs – the first Russian monarch to do so since the seventeenth century. Although the main forum for such experiments was Moscow, nonetheless he built a romantic wooden cottage in the Russian style in the park of Peterhof. However, the main thrust of his building in St. Petersburg remained in a style which fitted well into the unified framework of the city – the Marinsky Palace and the Alexander column both date from his reign.

Through his desire to protect the country from the destabilising contagion of dangerous ideas – the legacy of the French Revolution – the 'Iron Tsar' presided over a period of stagnation, bequeathing to his successor a number of problems he could not afford to ignore. The credit for the modernisation of Russia goes to Alexander II, 'the Liberator' (1855–81), who, although far less resolute than his awesome father, ruled in a time of great reforms, the most far-reaching of which was the liberation of the serfs in 1861. He inherited an Empire which was militarily defeated and economically backward, and instigated an industrial revolution which coincided with an agrarian one. Russian development was painful but attended by brilliant practical results. The artistic climate likewise was changing, and evidence of the shift in emphasis may be discerned in the architecture and the cultural life of the capital. From this time Imperial initiative ceases to be of primary importance. The descendants of Peter's Westernised elite, the intelligentsia appeared as a small but politically aggressive group adrift from the rest of society and crushed between the monarchy and the masses. Not all educated classes belonged to the intelligentsia but those who did were united by a common consensus; there was something profoundly religious in their make-up, although they professed atheism. They idealised the Russian peasant, identified with his lot, and aimed to serve him, but their Westernisation had alienated them from the masses and they felt the interests of the Russian people could best be served by converting them from their traditional structure of beliefs, their adherence to the Orthodox tradition and their veneration for the Tsar, all of which were a focus for their sense of unity.

In the summer of 1874, gangs of young Russians dressed as peasants went among the people, imitating their speech and aiming to share the burden of their labour. These emissaries of the intelligentsia were not well received by the peasantry – the movement ended in fiasco and deportation by the police. The sad consequences of Peter's schism – of the lack of organic unity in Russian life – were becoming apparent.

This tragic farce only served to accentuate the alienation of the intelligentsia and their sense of common identity. More and more the object of their detestation, the source of all evil, was the bureaucracy and the Autocratic system. Russian life was now in crisis. It was not simply that the style of St. Petersburg was now outmoded in terms of current taste, but that beauty itself had no relevance to a life that was dominated by the problem of Russia's backwardness and with the degraded state of the peasantry, which had just emerged from serfdom. Under these sombre shadows, Russia was reacting to the simultaneous impact of an agrarian and an industrial revolution. The changes entailed hardship, but they were accompanied by brilliant practical results.

There was nothing specifically Russian about St. Petersburg, at least in its inception, but the nineteenth-century writer and thinker Herzen considered that the genius of Pushkin's writing was the first indigenous creative response to Peter's revolution; Pushkin laid the foundation of a literary tradition which, in its interpretation of Western culture, is essentially Russian. The poet himself alluded to the quickening challenge of the changes. 'In a single decade,' he wrote, 'we shall experience what formerly absorbed half a century.' It was Falconet's monument which inspired Pushkin to write his most significant masterpiece, *The Bronze Horseman*, which is moreover an elegy on the destiny of Russia. It has been called the most passionate and the most noble anthem to the magnificence of St. Petersburg and to the glory of Peter, but in Peter's humble adversary the poem also evokes the human cost of his creation.

For Slavophiles, the true basis of Russian social and cultural life was to be found in its Orthodox faith and the traditions of its people. Russia could only evolve if it remained true to its own roots. Peter for them was a destroyer and his pseudomorphic creation, Petersburg, a foreign imposition. Khomiakov refers to it in 1832 as 'a granite desert, proud of its dead beauty', and Gogol declared that 'Russia has need of Moscow; Petersburg has need of Russia . . . a city where everything is of stone, the houses, the trees and the inhabitants', while the Russophobe French diplomat, de Custine, wrote in 1838 that 'nobody believes any more in the durability of this wonderful capital'. It is said that the poet Lermontov was accustomed to doodle the commemorative column of Alexander emerging above a raging flood. Vladimir Weidlé

comments, in *Russia Absent and Present*, that Dostoevsky never ceased to love Petersburg: 'He has described it and its atmosphere in an unforgettable way, and yet this attitude towards the city changed with the changing taste of his generation. In 1847 he contradicts the opinion of de Custine, stating that the city is the head and heart of Russia, that it is still under construction, that Peter's concept has not yet been fully realised . . . Fifteen years later, his opinion had changed, for in 1876 he expresses himself astonished that the Austrian ambassador found Petersburg beautiful.' (This is possibly most easily explained by remembering that the dominant architectural style of the city fell outside the circle of current fashion.) 'These different methods of looking at Petersburg in the course of time are important because through them one perceives the destiny of modern Russia. As we observe how, through Dostoevsky, increasingly the city assumes the aspect of an illusion, of a mirage which will disperse one day like a fog, leaving, as one reads in *Raw Youth*, only the Finnish swamp at the centre of which rears up the Bronze Horseman on its base. From this, one can be sure that what he thinks of the capital, he also thinks of the Empire.'

In 1863 an event took place in the Imperial Academy of Petersburg which helped to mould the aesthetics of the mid-nineteenth century into an organised artistic movement. While the Academy upheld unfashionable principles of romanticism and classicism, the students, infected by the radical critic Chernishevsky, whose book, *The Aesthetic Relationship of Art to Reality*, published in the first year of the new reign, set out to prove that 'reality is superior to its imitation in art', and found themselves in opposition to the institution's outmoded conventions. Fourteen students walked out of the Academy in protest against the theme set for a gold medal competition, 'The Feast of the Gods in Valhalla'. Inspired by this example, several Academy rebels organised a series of travelling exhibitions, in which, from 1872 onwards, their work was regularly displayed in provincial towns. In this way they sought to familiarise the public with the social content of their work and identified themselves with the popular movement headed by the intelligentsia. These artists, who became known as 'the Wanderers', established the aesthetic criteria which remained unchallenged until the emergence of the World of Art group in the 1890s.

By the last decade of the nineteenth century, the epoch dominated by the aesthetic ideals of the Wanderers had drawn to a close. After the murder of Alexander II the preoccupation with terrorism and the absorption of the intelligentsia in some of the more turgid manifestations of German philosophic thought were also dying away. Russia appeared to be entering calmer waters, and the star of St. Petersburg was once more rising. In fact, it was one of the contributions of the World of Art group that its leaders, among them Benois, Somov and Dobuzhinsky, rediscovered the beauty of the capital long despised by the generation of the 1870s and '80s. Most of the photographs here are of this period. They bring alive the era that Benois, Karsavina and others so vividly recall in their memoirs. Of course, what we cannot see are the colours – the sapphire-blue of the coachmen's coats, the scarlet liveries of the postilions of the court carriages, the cinnamon-coloured clothes, laced with silver, of the Circassian sweepers on the Palace quay, the bright booths of the fairgrounds and the ochres, deep reds, blues and greens of the buildings rising behind the pink granite quays. All these things brought their influence to bear on the artists of the period and stimulated their sense of theatre. Something of the energy, drama and excitement is apparent in the street scenes.

The accelerated pace of Russian life which had been rising to a crescendo, as predicted by Pushkin, reached its creative climax during the Silver Age. Painting, writing, poetry and even conversation were now fraught with the same measure of feverish excitement, the one stimulating the other, but with painting, often in the service of the theatre, in the lead. It seemed that the capital was heading for a bright future. Evolution, adaptation and change, inspired creative achievement affected every aspect of life. Its economy gave reason to believe that Russia would shortly overtake America as an industrialised nation. Its arts provoked the admiration of Europe, its literature and music were in the forefront of innovation. Yet in this Symbolist age there were also some gloomy forebodings. Pessimism was highlighted by the tragic events of 1905. Lacking the firm leadership of Alexander III, the intrigues of a clique who had the Emperor's ear led to a far Eastern adventure which resulted in a war with another rising nation, Japan. As often happens in Russian history, external events precipitated serious complications at home.

The humiliating result of the conflict sparked off internal unrest, in which it became apparent for the first time that broad sections of the population were disaffected. The government maintained its grip on events by firm action and concessions to those groups with real grievances. Having achieved their aspirations, and savoured the discomforts, the dislocation of life and the breakdown of communications brought by revolution, the majority of the public were content to return to normal life. Thereafter the appointment of Stolypin as premier – a man simultaneously ruthless in the suppression of any remaining sedition and dedicated to a policy of dramatic and radical reform in order to create a strong Russia – promised to

eradicate much discontent. But these reforms needed time to take hold. For some, the events of 1905 can be interpreted as a dress rehearsal for 1917, but it is also possible to view the subsequent evolution and development as a guarantee that the prospect of revolution was receding. Those who aspired to see Russia evolve as a parliamentary democracy saw the establishment of the *Duma* as hope of evolution. Petersburg served as a backdrop to all these events. The pattern of life was changing.

At the same time the city became a little more Russian, both because the architectural models it provided had passed into a Russian vernacular and were being interpreted on a more homely scale throughout the Empire and also because there was an influx of peasants who lived in the same style in the suburbs of the city as they had in their villages. The Slavophile aspirations of Alexander III and his son Nicholas II caused a number of buildings to be erected in an uncompromisingly Russian style, which stood out strangely against the neo-classical framework of the city.

The first and most conspicuous of these is the Church of the Saviour on the Blood built between 1883 and 1907. After 1905, other churches followed on the personal initiative of Nicholas – churches to commemorate the victims of the war in Japan, to mark the Romanov tercentenary of 1913, and other such events. This new departure did not mean a break with neo-classicism; on the eve of the outbreak of the First World War and under the impact of interest in the World of Art group, many fine buildings were commissioned in the revived neo-classical style.

All things were cut short by the outbreak of war, which, while the debilitating struggle between the government and the liberal opposition continued, imposed burdens on the country under the strain of which it broke down. The Tsar, as he stood on the balcony of the Winter Palace to acknowledge the deafening cheers of his people, did not share the crowd's hysterical elation. For a time, hatred of the enemy brought consensus as in the past, and all united around the sovereign. There had always been a strong German presence in Petersburg, playing a role both in trade and in the civil service, but now anyone who spoke German was liable to be lynched, or at the very least arrested. The name of St. Petersburg, actually Dutch in origin, was Russified to Petrograd. Its era as an Imperial city was drawing to a close.

Chapter 1

THE CITY

For the European traveller, St. Petersburg was usually the point of arrival in Russia, reached by a train journey via Berlin. After passing the neat Prussian homesteads and changing to a wider gauge train there was the slow progress of the Russian express, from the windows of which one saw a monotonous sequence of birch trees, marshes and the occasional village, more rambling and without the prim sobriety of its German counterparts.

Meriel Buchanan writes well about her first impression of Russia and her capital in 1910 – 'behind us lay the Europe that was familiar, before us lay a land strange and unknown'. Her father was the British ambassador, so their reception was formal: someone gave her mother flowers and the Imperial waiting room was opened for the family's use. Meriel had a confused impression of men in uniform, hurrying porters 'and most of all, of a smell, penetrating, all-pervading, hanging like a cloud over the crowded hall, following us into the quiet of the Imperial waiting room'. She and her party dined on marvellous hors d'oeuvres, steaming cabbage soup, and fish baked in pastry and stuffed with rice and hard-boiled eggs. But she remained perplexed by the curious smell. When she asked the Tartar waiter what it was, he replied that he did not notice it, and in time she, too, became accustomed to it, for it was in every shop and every public building, made up, so she thought, 'chiefly of leather, of sheepskin coats, of cabbage soup and sunflower oil'. Petersburg appeared a grey city that day: 'its wide streets (were) covered with dirty, half-melting snow and crowds muffled in heavy coats ... regarding the sleepy expression of the coachmen in their thick, wadded blue dressing gowns, one asked, could this still be Europe?'

The most obvious place to stay in St. Petersburg, then as now, was the Hôtel de l'Europe, where travellers have put up since the 1860s, on the corner of Nevsky Prospekt with easy access to the smartest shops and to *Gostinni Dvor*, the covered market reminiscent of the great bazaars of the orient, and conveniently situated close to the recently opened Alexander III Museum. Expensive and fashionable, everything was billed separately, and a bath cost the equivalent of three shillings and sixpence. Every private house and hotel had swarms of servants. In 1900 the visiting English M.P. Henry Norman wrote, in evident disgruntlement, that they expected a tip if they so much as took your hat, 'fivepence is little enough, and half-a-crown evidences no gratitude'. He remarked that the more homelike Hôtel de France was the place to see 'true Petersburg'. The Hôtel d'Angleterre, opposite St. Isaac's Cathedral, was more modest, and the Astoria, opened nearby at the turn of the century, more luxurious, its comfortable rooms decorated in the latest neo-Grecian style. Every traveller noticed that hotels and private houses alike were efficiently heated – to an extent that the Englishman with his woollen underclothes was not prepared for.

Nevsky Prospekt offered brightly lit shop windows to the gaze of the passer by. The façades were often painted with pictures of the goods inside – coats and trousers for a tailor; saws and hammers for an ironmonger and pyramids of fruit for a greengrocer (see page 27). *Gostinni Dvor*, the Westernised version of the great Eastern bazaars, sold similar exotic wares, among them scent, of which foreigners noticed that Russians made more lavish use than Western Europeans, and fine textiles, some of them antique. When Diaghilev was working on a performance of *Boris Godonuv*, the pearl-embroidered headdresses known as *kokoshniki* and the brightly coloured traditional dresses (*sarafani*) for many of the costumes could still be bought cheaply enough in the market. For those interested in articles of a more up-to-date and European character, Druces sold imported goods – Floris bath essence, Atkinson's salts, chintzes and Scotch tweed – and Aleksandre and Knoop, the Petersburg counterparts to Asprey's, imported elegant knick-knacks. But no European jeweller had the prestige of Fabergé, whose windows on Morskaya Street always offered a visual treat. Even his smallest products – his tiny hardstone animals – were imbued with a liveliness and a humour that made them different from the merely kitsch fantasies of inferior craftsmen. He did not invariably use expensive materials; his art was more subtle. At Easter especially his clients appreciated his ingenuity. He sold enamelled eggs, the size of a little finger nail, to be worn on Easter night and over the following forty days. Every year he was commissioned to produce a larger pair of Easter eggs for the Emperor – one for his consort and the other for his mother. He had *carte blanche* in designing these: they remained a surprise until delivered.

As in any city, much socialising took place at home. Russian hospitality demanded that the arrival of guests should be the signal for the bringing out of steaming samovars, the serving of tea and the laying out of food. This was customary in all classes of household, from the cramped flats on the fourth or sixth floors where clerks drank tea from glasses to the elegant town houses where salons were held, and the palaces of the great, where the company dined at small tables, served *à la Russe* by waiters.

The restaurants of the capital were plentiful and popular, but there was no such thing as a bar or pub, although there were automatic buffets where it was possible to drink on the penny-in-the-slot principle, and children were sent to the shops with empty bottles and kopeks to bring vodka home. Most of the restaurants offered entertainment of one sort or another, whether gypsy singers or, less appealing, mechanical organs with drums and cymbals, which could be run by electricity and played raucously throughout the day. The theatres and music halls were also much frequented and many private concerts where held in houses and at the clubs – notably at the Circle of the Nobility, a club for the upper classes, where it was not the done thing to applaud: the quality of the silence after a performance revealed the degree of its success. There were occasionally even balls at the Winter Palace to which the ordinary townsfolk of the capital, if they could afford a frockcoat, were admitted.

Life in St. Petersburg revolved around the seasons, the feastdays and the namedays. Friends exchanged visits at Christmas, admired the decorated trees and went for sleigh drives on the mile-wide frozen river past the lighted

Previous page: Nevsky Prospekt, the main thoroughfare through the city, taken in 1900. The building set back from the street is St. Catherine's, the principal Catholic church in St. Petersburg – there were so many churches of different faiths along Nevsky that it was nicknamed 'Toleration Street'. Built to the design of Jean Vallin de la Mothe, but completed by Rinaldi, St. Catherine's was consecrated on 9 March 1762. Most Catholics in the city were of French and Polish origin, and Stanislaus Poniatovsky, the last king of Poland, and the French general, Jean Victor Moreau, are both buried here.

windows of the palaces on the embankment. For the two weeks of the festival Lapps arrived from the northern wastes of the grand Duchy of Finland and set up camp in the middle of the river in their shelters covered with animal skins. They traded furs and offered rides in their reindeer-driven sledges.

Officially the Russian social season began with the Christmas bazaar at the Circle of the Nobility, organised by the Grand Duchess Maria Pavlovna, which lasted for four days from two in the afternoon until midnight. After Christmas, balls and dances were held until Lent. Unmarried girls did not attend the same balls or share the same partners as those who were married. The *bals blancs* were held especially for the former and were run strictly according to conventional etiquette. It was not the custom to have an orchestra but as a survival from an earlier period there was an old grey-haired *tappeur*, who played the piano while rows of formidable chaperones, dressed in black and seated on gilt chairs, scrutinised their charges, and a master of ceremonies saw that no girl was left out. The two-step was considered improper, there were never many waltzes and the Emperor had forbidden officers in uniform to dance the one-step or the tango, so most of the evening was taken up by endless quadrilles orchestrated by the master of ceremonies.

The week of *Maslenitsa* (Shrovetide) brought more fairs and excursions. From the mid-nineteenth century the fairs were held on a site near the Winter Palace, with puppeteers, swings, performing bears and barrel organs, pedlars, and sellers of pies and spiced drinks. There were also several circuses in the city, of which the best known was the Ciniselli on the Fantanka Embankment. The chief attraction here was a woman who put her head into a crocodile's mouth. The police tried to forbid the act as too dangerous, but the woman begged to be allowed to continue to earn her living – and was eventually eaten by the crocodile.

In the first week of Lent the atmosphere in the city became sober. Meat could no longer be bought in the butchers' shops, the Emperor and Empress left the capital for the seclusion of their estate at Gatchina, and the ancient canon of St. Andrew of Crete was recited in the churches, where the clergy wore only black. The theatres closed – they could not compete with the liturgical drama being enacted in the city's churches. The cycle ended with the joyous celebration of Easter, coinciding with spring, season of rebirth and renewal.

For the serious-minded visitor the museums of St. Petersburg were many and extraordinarily various. The Hermitage with its unrivalled collection of Dutch and Italian masters could be visited, and its newest acquisition admired – a Madonna by Leonardo, which had belonged to Leonty Benois, been authenticated by his brother, the artist Alexander, and bought by the Tsar for his collection on the advice of his close friend, Zinaida Yusupova. If the Imperial family were not in residence it was also possible to visit the Winter Palace between the hours of eleven and three. Visitors were required to show cards of admission obtained from the office of the chief of the Palace police to the left of the entrance facing the Alexander column. Highlights of such a visit were the Romanov gallery, its array of dynastic portraits beginning with the Patriarch Philaret, father of the first Romanov Tsar; the St. George Salon in white and gold, which was the throne room of the Palace; a chamber where the Imperial crown jewels, unrivalled in Europe, were displayed; and the furnished apartments of a succession of Emperors and Empresses each of which reflected their individual tastes and the fashions of their time.

The junction of Nevsky Prospekt and Bolshaya Morskaya. The building on the corner is on the site of a house which once belonged to Prince Vasilchikov, master of the Imperial hunt in the 1830s. It was rebuilt in the 1880s. The premises of the ladies' tailor, Chernyshev, are on the first floor, and display an impressive number of Imperial and Royal warrants, including the arms of the Grand Duchess Maria Pavlovna, and the Royal Arms of Greece (Queen Olga was born a Russian Grand Duchess). On the ground floor Thonet, the Viennese furniture manufacturer and the first to produce popular bentwood furniture, displays the Imperial Austrian warrant over his shop. Wicker furniture is piled in the window, with very little attempt at a window display. It was quite common to have several shops in the same building, one in the basement, another on the ground floor, a third on the first floor and so on. Policemen stand on the right and left of the picture.

Shops on Nevsky Prospekt. Adolphe's hairdressers has a fine window display of wigs and hair accessories, and there are separate entrances for the ladies' and gentlemen's shops.

Right: Another view of Nevsky, taken in 1913. On the right, the electrically lit sign of the *Passage* Theatre, where Russian operetta and light comedies were performed. On the left is the covered bazaar of *Gostinni Dvor*, or Merchants' Row, first built towards the end of the eighteenth century by Vallin de la Mothe, but completely remodelled at the end of the nineteenth century, and beyond it the tower of the *duma* or city council. In the middle distance, on the right-hand side of the street, one can make out the curious *fin-de-siècle* globe-crowned dome of the Singer building. This housed the Singer sewing-machine shop on the ground floor (see page 26).

Repairing the overhead tram wires. This photograph, taken by Bulla in 1908, shows the wooden scaffolding carts used for street repairs. Electric trams were first introduced to the city in 1907.

Opposite: The department store of Yeliseev Brothers, the Fortnum and Mason of St. Petersburg, at 56 Nevsky Prospekt. Built between 1902 and 1907, the façades are decorated with bronzes and large panels of stained glass. Principally a delicatessen, there were trade stores on the ground floor, a concert hall on the second, and a foyer, with buffets, lounges and a space for small concerts and chamber music, on the third. The millionaire Yeliseev family also had a similar store on Tverskaya Street in Moscow.

Opposite: A view of Nevsky Prospekt taken from an upper window. This photograph gives some sense of the bustle and the crowds along Nevsky. In the centre distance one can see the dome of the Kazan Cathedral. Nevsky is intersected by three canals and is two-and-three-quarter miles long. It leads from the Admiralty at its northern end to the Alexander Nevsky monastery, becoming progressively less smart as it winds south-east.

Nevsky taken in 1896 by Bulla, the fashionable Petersburg photographer. The buildings are decorated with white, red and blue Russian tricolours to celebrate the coronation of Nicholas II which took place in Moscow in the same year. On the right is a false wooden front, put up to conceal construction work behind it. The trams are advertising Blüchel cocoa, and the heavily decorated shop on the centre left is called 'The World of Electricity'.

View down Nevsky Prospekt towards Znamenskaya Square, so named after the Icon of the Virgin of the Sign. On the right, an open market is trading in front of *Gostinni Dvor*, the buildings of which form an irregular quadrangle, with façades on Nevsky, Sadovaya Prospekt, Chernishev Lane and Duma Prospekt. At the turn of the century around five thousand people worked there, and the arcades of the first and second floors were a favourite promenade for Petersburg residents. Baedeker notes that these arcades contained about two hundred shops, 'which, however, are less elegant than the other shops of the Nevski' – other contemporaries observed that it was a good place to see all the national types of Petersburg and admired the wares: Russian leather slippers embroidered with silver and gold, furs, porcelain, stones and pearls.

Above: The 'Green' Bridge across the Moika Canal along Nevsky Prospekt. In the 1730s the first wooden drawbridges were built across the Moika. They were brightly painted and named according to their colours – yellow, red, green and blue. After 1777 the Green Bridge became known as the Politeisky (Police) Bridge because it was situated next to the house of the city's Chief of Police, Chicherin. Between 1806 and 1808 the bridge was replaced by a single-span structure of bolted cast-iron blocks, to the design of the architect V. I. Geste. The result was light but solid, with elegant wrought-iron work and lanterns, and stood the test of time well, and the pattern was much repeated in Petersburg in the 1820s and '30s. On 30 December 1883 the first electric power station began its operation from a barge alongside the bridge, lighting up Nevsky Prospekt from the Moika to the Fontanka Canals. On the extreme right of the picture one can see the corner of the palace of the Stroganov family, well-known patrons of the arts, designed by Rastrelli. A barge loaded with wood is moored alongside.

The *duma* tower decorated for the visit of the French president, Loubet, in 1913. A painted banner on the façade shows Notre Dame and St. Isaac's Cathedral, and busts of the Emperor and the President flank that of the Empress Alexandra on a small plinth.

The town hall, or *duma* building, built by Ferrari in 1802, with an unusual pentagonal tower. From the middle of the eighteenth century, the heads of the merchants' guilds of the city met on this site. The tower was used for the semaphore telegraph system which, in the middle of the nineteenth century, established communication between the Imperial residences of the Winter Palace and Gatchina, and Kronstadt, Vilnius and Warsaw. Balloons of different colours were flown from the tower to warn of imminent floods threatening the city. On the left is the small chapel of the Guslizky monastery, built in 1861 by the architect Gornostaev. It is situated in front of *Gostinni Dvor*, the façade of which can just be seen on the extreme left of the picture.

Opposite below: Newspaper vendors gathered around the steps of the *duma*. Among their wares are *Vecha*, *Petersburgskiye Vedomosti* (the *Petersburg News*, a large-circulation newspaper of rather conservative views) and *The Orator*.

Crowds are drawn to a demonstration in the window of the Singer sewing machine shop.

18 Nevsky Prospekt. This part of Nevsky was already well established by the mid-eighteenth century, and between 1812 and 1815 the buildings were substantially altered by the architect V. P. Stasov. During the first half of the nineteenth century the café of Wolf and Beranger was situated on this corner site, much frequented by artists and writers. It was here that the poet Pushkin became friendly with Danzas, who was to act as his second in the duel in which he died. By the beginning of the twentieth century, when this photograph was taken, F. Tremen, a German umbrella manufacturer, had his shop on the ground floor and the premises of the photographer Pavel Zhukov were at the top of the house. On the right, alongside the Catherine Canal, is a shop advertising fruit imported from the Crimea. The façade is painted with elaborate, fruit-filled urns.

Procession in Palace Square during
the celebrations of the tercentenary
of the Romanov dynasty in 1913.
The Tsar and the Tsarevich are in
the first carriage, and the Empresses
follow in closed carriages. The path
is lined with soldiers of the
Pavlovsky Regiment in their
distinctive headdresses, and in the
foreground one can see the
regimental banner embroidered with
the Holy Visage. The Palace is flying
the Imperial standard. Nicholas II
decided that events would be
commemorated as a Russian family
occasion by his visit down the Volga
to Kostromo and thence to Moscow,
but without any attendance by his
government. Prior to this journey
the Tsar and his family came from
their retreat at the Alexander Palace
at Tsarskoye Selo for the first time
since 1905 to stay for a few days at
the Winter Palace. On 6 March they
drove in state to the Kazan
Cathedral for a solemn service of
thanksgiving. All the high
functionaries of the Empire were
present, and troops lined the streets
through which the Imperial
procession was to pass. In her book,
*Behind the Veil at the Russian
Court*, Princess Radziwill recalls:
'The Emperor looked grave and
pale. He drove in an open carriage
with his little son seated beside him,
and when he entered the Cathedral a
Cossack from the escort took the
child in his arms and carried him
inside the church where he was
placed in a chair beside his mother.'
The white, pinched face of the boy
made a painful impression on the
spectators, who were now very
much aware that there was
something tragically wrong with the
child's health.

A summer procession passing the corner of the Winter Palace. The two Empresses, Maria Feodorovna and Alexandra Feodorovna, are accompanied by the Tsar on horseback.

The funeral cortège of the Grand Duke Konstantin Konstantinovich, en route to the Peter Paul Fortress in 1915. Grand ducal funerals were days of public mourning, and the lengthy procession made its way slowly across the city on foot. Konstantin Konstantinovich was remembered as a poet and an art patron; it was said that he lost the will to live after his son and his son-in-law perished in the Great War. Three more sons were shot in horrifying circumstances in 1919. The Grand Duke had lived a peaceful and patriarchal life, holding aloof from the grandeur of the court. His was the last Imperial State funeral in Russia.

Paving the Palace Embankment with wooden blocks. Wood pavements were first used in Petersburg in the 1820s, and in 1832 Nevsky Prospekt was laid with wooden planking from Palace Bridge to the Anichkov Palace. Such pavements required frequent routine repairs, but the materials and labour were cheap and they were much quieter than the rough stone paving. At the beginning of the twentieth century about twenty streets in St. Petersburg were still paved in this way. From right to left, the buildings on this part of the Embankment are Rastrelli's Winter Palace; the Small Hermitage; the old Hermitage, by Vallin de la Mothe, and the Hermitage Theatre, by Quarenghi. In the distance one can just see the Renaissance-style porch of the Palace of Grand Duke Vladimir (see page 108). Notice also the eighteenth-century pink granite quays lining the Embankment on the left, which were erected for Catherine II by Vallin de la Mothe.

Palace Embankment. On the right is the iron railing surrounding a garden first closed off by Nicholas II. The rooms on the first floor on the corner overlooking it were his private apartments, although they were seldom occupied by the Imperial couple after 1905.

A small food and produce stall.

Christmas trees for sale. The custom of decorating a tree for Christmas was imported to Russia, as it was to Britain, from Germany. The trees would have been brought in, like dairy and farm produce, from the villages around Petersburg.

A postcard stall. The wares ranged from pictures of the Imperial family, prominent society figures and portraits of actresses and music-hall stars to cheap reproductions of well-known works of art and sentimental genre scenes.

A stall selling caged birds.

Smolensk Prospekt, photographed by Bulla in 1900. Two wine shops and a photographer advertise their wares in this, a less smart area of the city.

The New York/*Pobeda* (Victory) bicycle shop on Malaya Morskaya. In the basement is a lighting shop selling candles and kerosene lamps. Other notices advertise life insurance and pawnbrokers.

Likhachov's wallpaper shop on Vasilievsky Island, decorated to commemorate the tercentenary of the dynasty in old Russian style, incorporating the Imperial double-headed eagle and the Romanov family arms of the griffin. The upper stories of the building advertise a dentist and a sewing-machine shop.

The covered market of *Apraxin Dvor*, located between Sadovaya Street and the Fontanka Canal. Named after the rich and noble Apraxin family, who originally owned a house on this site, the first trade market appeared here at the end of the eighteenth century. A fire in 1862 destroyed the wooden market and a new arcaded building was constructed of brick and stone the following year. At the beginning of the twentieth century more than six hundred stalls were housed here and the complex had one of the biggest cash turnovers of European markets, trading in furs, clothes, haberdashery, furniture, shoes, spices, food and wine.

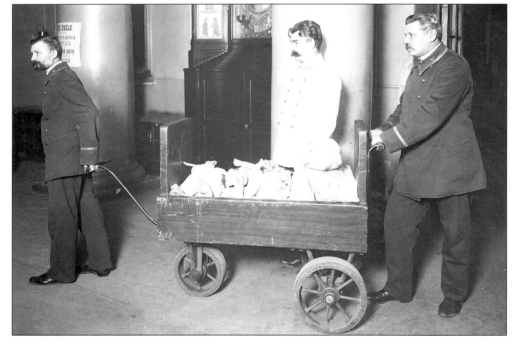

Above left: A doorman and a waiter posed outside the *Nadezhda* (Hope) Restaurant at the junction of Admiral and Voznesensky (Ascension) Prospekts. An ordinary, not particularly smart, restaurant for a middle-class clientele. The specialities of the day are shown on a white card in a glass panel to the left of the door. The waiters at this time were often of Tartar origin, as is the case here.

The transfer of gold at a bank. Three men are required – two porters to have charge of the trolley and a clerk to oversee proceedings. Gold was habitually transported in jars, tied up in cloth. Note the wooden stand containing icons in the background – most offices and workplaces had a *krasniy ugel* (icon corner) like this.

Above: A wine merchant's shop. The extravagant Art Nouveau light fitting and the illumination on the ceiling of the cellar place this picture at the turn of the century. Obviously a posed shot, three customers face the camera with the shop's manager.

A shop display of wine and liqueurs. Among the goods advertised are fruit liqueurs and flavoured vodkas from the Petersburg firm of Kalinkin.

Yegorov's baths were among the most luxurious in the capital. The amenities included a tented Moorish disrobing room, a pool ornamented with tiling, statuary, a decorative bridge and trailing greenery, and a sauna, where clients are being beaten with birch twigs to stimulate circulation. The attendants are uniformed in traditional Russian shirts with embroidered collars. There are individual cubicles in the sauna, and the room is equipped with a shower which operates from a tank above. All the men are Orthodox, for they wear the crosses which, first received at baptism, are thereafter always worn under their shirts.

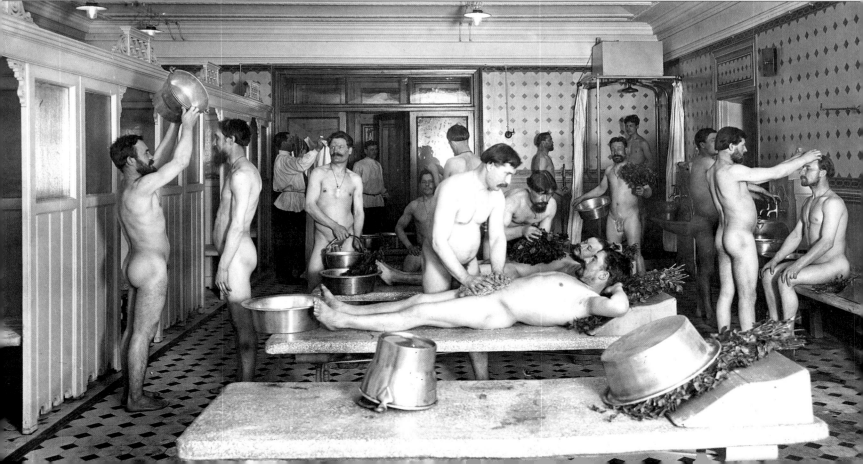

Porters unloading outside the Nicholas Railway Station on the direct line to Moscow in the south-east of the city, at the far end of Nevsky Prospekt. In the first picture they unload a cart under the supervision of a policeman, in the second, a porter collects the hampers and hatboxes from a horse-drawn cab. Both pictures are dated 1913.

The railway station for Tsarskoye Selo. In October 1837, the first railway from St. Petersburg through Tsarskoye Selo to Pavlovsk was opened here. The original wooden structure was replaced in 1850 by a stone building which was in its turn replaced in 1904 by this building, designed by the architect S. A. Brzozovsky, with characteristic Art Nouveau decoration applied to the façade.

Znamenskaya Square, looking towards Nevsky Prospekt from the Nicholas Railway station. In the centre of the square is the monument to Alexander III by Prince Pavel Trubetskoy. A competition was held to decide the design of the monument, and Trubetskoy's submission was chosen from a number, among which were designs by Beck, Beklemishev, Ober, Opekushin and Chizov, all distinguished sculptors of the period, by a jury headed by Nicholas II himself. The statue took five years to complete, and the casting a further year and a half. The base was constructed by the noted architect Fyodor Shekhtel of four colossal blocks of red granite held together without the use of any clamps or ties. The official inauguration, a picture of which is shown below, took place on 23 May 1909, and the statue was unveiled to an extremely mixed reception. As a rather stolid, ungraceful portrait it went against the prevailing fashion for more conventional heroic images, and it was widely mocked and criticised. However, the Dowager Empress liked it and kept a maquette of the original design in her study. In style it is reminiscent of representations of the *bogatyri*, the warrior heroes of ancient Russia.

Right: St. Isaac's Cathedral is of special significance for St. Petersburg. It commemorates the saint on whose nameday Peter the Great was born, Isaac of Dalmatia, in whose name five monarchs in succession had begun to build a cathedral. The present structure was begun in 1818 following a competition which was won by a total outsider, Ricard de Montferrand. He had submitted designs in the Chinese, Indian, Gothic and Byzantine styles – however, the ultimate result was one of the last great neo-classical buildings in Europe, modified and augmented over the years until it became somewhat ponderous.

Thousands of timber piles were required to strengthen the foundations deep in the capital's swampy soil. Forty-eight monolithic columns of granite had to be raised into position, the dome was constructed over iron ribs and no expense was spared to sheathe the interior with marbles, mosaics, and pillars veneered in precious materials.

Changing the guard at the monument to Nicholas I.

Opposite: The equestrian statue to Nicholas I Pavlovich, erected on Marinsky Square, facing St. Isaac's and with the Marinsky Palace behind it. Cast to the designs of the sculptor, Baron Klodt, and unveiled in 1859, the monument was particularly admired for the way in which the prancing horse is balanced, its weight resting only on the hind legs. The pedestal of granite and marble is embellished with portraits of the Emperor's wife and daughters as Justice, Strength, Wisdom and Faith. There are also four bas reliefs depicting key events from the reign.

Test driving a new lorry in 1901 on Senate
Square. Falconet's statue can be seen in the
background.

Opposite: The main entrance arch of the Admiralty. The first Admiralty building was constructed by Peter the Great in 1704, and was
essentially both dockyard and fortress, protected by ramparts and a moat. Between 1806 and 1823 the tower with its gilded steeple was
built to the design of the architect A. D. Zakharov. The arch is flanked by two limestone sculptural groups by Schedrin, each comprising
three nymphs supporting a globe. Until 1844 ships were still built at the Admiralty, and Peter's city bristled with the masts of ships, the
smell of tar evoking his love affair with Amsterdam; after 1844, it became redundant as a dockyard, but the Naval Department was still
housed in the buildings.

Left: Flooding in St. Petersburg in 1903. Between the foundation of the city and the beginning of the twentieth century, St. Petersburg was flooded over two hundred times, and floods were dreaded there in the way that other cities dread fire. It was the custom to fire cannon to warn people living in basements to get out. Augustus Hare, writing in the 1890s, records that when the first guns were heard, they attracted no attention, 'it is "only an inundation"', but that at the second volley, horses were moved from the stables in the lower town and other precautions were taken. One of the great floods is commemorated in Pushkin's poem, *The Bronze Horseman*. Here, the Krukhov Canal has overflowed its banks. The Marinsky Theatre is in the centre of the picture.

Above: Electric tramlines laid on the frozen Neva. At the end of the nineteenth century, horse trams were one of the main means of public transport in Petersburg. They were managed by a private company which had concluded a profitable contract with the city *duma* giving it the exclusive rights to ground transport for twenty-five years, and which refused to give way to electric trams. However, the contract naturally said nothing about water or ice, and rival companies laid tramlines on the Neva as soon as it froze over. These tramways were resumed every winter, but it was not until 1907 that the first electric trams appeared on the streets of the capital.

Two sailors row past a flooded church.

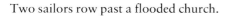

Left: The opening, in 1911, of the Okhtinsky Bridge across the Neva. Named for Peter the Great, the bridge was designed by the architect Apishkov with the engineer, Krivoshein, and with Leonid Benois, brother of the leading member of the World of Art group, Alexander, acting as architectural consultant. It was admired as a prodigious feat of engineering.

Below left: Preobrazhensky (Transfiguration) Square on a national holiday. A large fruit and flower market was regularly held here. In the background one can see the portico of the Church of the Transfiguration (see page 56). The elegant eagles on the gateposts have lowered wings, an indication that they were designed at the beginning of the nineteenth century.

Below: The 'Egyptian' chain bridge across the Fontanka Canal, constructed in 1826. The decorative detail of the columns and portals are in an Egyptian style, admired during the early nineteenth century. The structure collapsed while a cavalry squadron was crossing. The disaster encouraged designers to abandon the use of chain-metal supports in favour of multi-stranded cables.

Opposite above: The Tsar's family descend the steps to their barge on Petrovsky Embankment, escorted by Count Friederickes (see page 110). The building in the background is the palace of Grand Duke Nikolai Nikolaevich. The embankment is ornamented with a stone lion, brought from Manchuria in 1907.

Opposite below: Crossing the Nicholas Bridge from Vasilievsky Island in winter. On the left is a small chapel dedicated to St. Nicholas, favourite saint of Russia. It contained a mosaic image of the saint, a replica of a portrait in the church of St. Nicholas at Bari, where he is buried. Such small chapels and wayside shrines were found throughout the city.

Above: View from the steps of the stock exchange across to the English Embankment. In the centre is one of the Rostral columns, modelled on Roman columns mounted with trophies, and built in the early nineteenth century to serve as signal towers. They are decorated with symbolic ships' prows and monumental figures representing the four great Russian rivers – the Neva, the Volga, the Dnieper and the Volkhov.

Peter the Great's log cabin on the Petrovsky Embankment is the oldest building in the capital. It was constructed in three days in 1703, and painted to simulate brickwork in line with Peter's aim to create a city of brick and stucco on the model of Amsterdam. Later, Peter, personally indifferent to grandeur to the point where he had to borrow the house of his favourite, Menshikov, for state occasions, preserved the building under a timber shell in recognition of its historical importance. Later still it was clad in brick and served as a chapel where the celebrated Icon of the Holy Visage was enshrined (see page 62).

The Kazan Cathedral was built between 1801 and 1811 from designs by Voronikhin. Although the choice of architect was intended to make the project an all-Russian one the semi-circular colonnade instantly recalls comparison with Bernini's entrance to St. Peter's in Rome. The Cathedral held one of several versions of the miracle-working icon of the Virgin of Kazan and was intimately associated with many events in the life of the capital; for example, the court repaired here during the celebrations of the tercentenary of 1913, and it was here that the Tsar came to pray at the outbreak of the Great War.

The Fortress of St. Peter and St. Paul, above, which contains the Cathedral of the same name dates back to the time of Peter. The slender tower which is such a feature of the Petersburg skyline reflected Peter's admiration for Dutch Baroque. Here Peter and all subsequent Autocrats (with the exception of Peter II, who died in Moscow) lie buried. There are thirty white marble tombs simply inscribed with names of the monarchs and their consorts and clad with icons and embroidered cloths, with stands for candles placed nearby. The illustration on the right shows the tombs of Alexander II and his consort, designed by Gun. They stand out because they are fashioned from green-grey jasper from the Altai mountains and pink and black rhodonite from the Urals. They took more than ten years to complete at the celebrated Peterhof lapidary workshop and were only erected in their final form in 1906.

The Church of the Transfiguration (Preobrazhenie), completed in 1829 to the design of Stasov, served the prestigious Preobrazhensky Regiment. The oldest guards regiment, it was founded by Peter the Great in the village of Preobrazhenskoye near Moscow in 1687. It was encircled by a cast-iron fence made from Turkish cannon captured during the Russo-Turkish war of 1828. The boundary posts were formed from groups of three cannon surmounted by crowned and gilded double-headed eagles. The church contained regimental trophies such as flags and the keys of captured cities.

The Trinity Cathedral, also built by Stasov, was the church of another celebrated regiment, the Ismailovsky. It was built between 1827 and 1835 on the initiative of Maria Feodorovna, the widowed consort of Paul. On this site, it is said, Peter married his Empress, Catherine, in an earlier wooden chapel. The star-spangled blue domes are a landmark of the city. In front of the Cathedral stands Grimm's monument, a cast-iron Corinthian column incorporating captured cannon and surmounted by a bronze Victory. It was erected in 1886 to commemorate the Turkish war of 1877–88.

The Church of the Resurrection, popularly known as the Saviour on the Blood, was raised over the spot where Alexander II fell victim to a terrorist attack on the quay of the Catherine Canal. The place was at first marked by a wooden chapel while a competition was held to raise a suitable monument which, in accordance with the taste of Alexander III, was conceived in Russian style. The successful candidate was Parland and the construction, which began in the coronation year of 1883, was not completed until 1907. The materials used for this assertive statement of Slavophilism right in the heart of classical St. Petersburg were lavish. There are 7,000 square metres of mosaic covering the interior and exterior surfaces to produce a carpet-like effect. In the interior a baldequin of semi-precious stone was raised above the bloodstained cobbles.

Opposite: The Lutheran church of St. Peter's on Nevsky Prospekt. Designed by Bryullov and built in 1838, it was augmented between 1909 and 1910. From its inception Petersburg had a large foreign colony in which Germans especially were prominent. The famous German school, the *Peterschule* was located just behind St. Peter's.

Opposite below left: The delicate church of the Saviour on the Waters, accurately reproducing features of twelfth-century Suzdalian architecture, commemorates soldiers and sailors who lost their lives during the war with Japan in 1904.

Opposite below right: During the first decade of the twentieth century the research of a new generation gave rise to a fresh reworking of old Russian forms. In contrast to the overloaded ornament superimposed on such buildings as the Church of the Saviour on the Blood, the new movement was concerned with space and volume, simple ornament was used to punctuate the structure and to enhance the liturgical function of the space. Many buildings in this style originated in the interest and personal patronage of the Imperial family. The Church of the Fedorovskaya – named for the venerable icon of the Mother of God with which Martha blessed her son, Michael, upon his accession as the first Romanov – was built at Tsarskoye Selo as part of an architectural complex completed in 1912 by the architect Pokrovsky. The church reveals clean, simplified lines and the exaggerated perspectives characteristic of the *fin-de siècle*. The façades are decorated with mosaics and the interior held the Imperial family's rare personal collection of ancient icons. The church held a special meaning for the family of Nicholas II.

Above right: The church of Chesme, erected on the outskirts of the capital on the route to Tsarskoye Selo, was commissioned by Catherine the Great from the architect Felten to commemorate the brilliant victory of the Russian fleet over the Ottomans at the bay of Chesme in March 1770. Its exotic style reflects a search for new forms which are manifest in a number of buildings erected by Catherine. The jewel-like delicacy of the structure was so admired that two replicas were built elsewhere in the Empire. Close by is a palace of the same name, and a small cemetery for war veterans and for Knights of the Order of St. George.

Right: The Buddhist temple on Staraya Derevnaya, built on the initiative of the Dalai Lama, who, having visited St. Petersburg, kept a permanent personal representative in the city. Completed to the design of the architect Baranovsky in 1915, the project was organised by a committee of dedicated orientalists, including the painter Roerich. A hostel for monks and their guests was built nearby.

A panoramic view of the city from Vasilievsky Island in 1903, across the Neva towards the English Embankment, named after the large English community in that district.

Right: Sennaya (Haymarket) Square, situated on the busy main Petersburg–Moscow road. A haymarket had been held here from the 1730s, but by the end of the century it was trading in meat, fish, vegetables and fruit. Consisting of four large buildings designed by Kitner it housed some five hundred stalls. Behind is the Church of the Dormition, built with donations from the rich merchant Savva Yakovlev. Opposite is a guard-house of the city, built in 1820 by the architect Beretti.

Clergy conveying the Icon of the Holy Visage to be used in a *molebin* during the celebrations of the bicentenary of St. Petersburg in May 1903. The icon was kept in the chapel which had originally been Peter the Great's log cabin, on Petrovsky Embankment, and was brought by boat to the various ceremonies in the city in which it was used.

A flotilla of decorated yachts on the Neva in May 1903 celebrate the bicentenary of St. Petersburg. The spit of Vasilievsky Island can be seen in the background. The austerely elegant building with Doric columns is the stock exchange, designed in 1804 by the French architect Thomon.

A horse tram crossing the Palace Bridge in the winter of 1903.

Left and below: The inauguration of the Troitsky (Trinity) Bridge across the Neva during the celebration of the bicentenary of St. Petersburg in May 1903. The ceremony was attended by the Emperor, the two Empresses and the mayor P. M. Delyanov. A *molebin*, a short religious ceremony to invoke a blessing, marks the opening. A mitred metropolitan raises his hand in benediction, while a deacon swings a censer.

The French President, Poincaré, is conducted by Cossacks down Nevsky Prospekt during his state visit in 1914. The Anichkov Palace, residence of the Emperor's mother, looms in the background. On the extreme left is the Beloselsky Palace, built by Stackenschneider in the mid-nineteenth century and successively occupied by Grand Dukes Sergei, Paul and Dmitri Pavlovich.

The Anichkov Palace, built in the 1740s, was remodelled on a number of occasions. Empress Elizabeth gave it to her favourite, Count Razumovsky, who some say was also her husband. Later Catherine conferred it on her favourite, the brilliant statesman Potyomkin. During the nineteenth century the Palace was customarily the residence of the heir. Alexander III, having occupied it as Tsarevich, never moved into the Winter Palace after his accession. His widow, Maria Feodorovna, continued to live here during her son's reign.

A queue for lottery tickets in the Summer Garden in 1911. Here, behind an elegant railing, are the small Summer Pavilion of Peter and a number of memorable sculptures. The garden was a favourite meeting place for strollers, among whom Nicholas I and Alexander II were regularly to be seen.

Petrovsky Park on a Sunday. The caps and
headscarves indicate that most of the
strollers are working class. Some are taking
their seats for an open-air concert. There
were many open-air stages in the parks of
the city, where a wide variety of
entertainment – popular comedy, operettas
and plays – were performed.

The audience at one of the open-air theatres
in Petrovsky Park.

Right: A tea pavilion, designed in the vernacular Russian style with characteristic geometric wooden fretwork, and run by the influential Petersburg Temperance Society.

Below: Easter festivities. The warehouse-like building is the popular 'Theatre for All', showing a play about the campaigns of General Suvorov in the time of Catherine the Great, and 'Scenes of Village Life', a comedy. Across the river, one can see a church being built in the revived Russian style fashionable at the beginning of the twentieth century.

One of the first buses in St. Petersburg. The service was organised in 1907 by the businessman V. A. Ivanov.

Car crash on the Moika Embankment. A crowd looks on as firemen retrieve the vehicle with ropes. In the background is the fashionable Medved (Bear) Restaurant much frequented by theatregoers.

Collecting household rubbish from one of the specially designed towers where it was deposited.

Registration at the entrance to a horse auction. The sale is of draught rather than riding horses. Horse markets were held weekly in a number of locations.

Street scene in one of the poorer districts. The shops include a seller of *kvas* (a popular traditional drink, a kind of mild beer made from fermented rye bread), a canteen and a public bath, advertised as 'family' or communal baths. Two uniformed firemen are seen in the foreground and in the distance, across the river, are factory chimneys.

Opposite: A switchback ride (a new development arising out of the Russian obsession with slides and snow mountains, enjoyed by all classes) on the Field of Mars (*Marsovo Polye*), the Imperial drill ground. The great military parades of all regiments which took place at the end of April were held here between 1818 and the end of the nineteenth century. Fairs continued to be held here on feastdays and holidays.

A new type of ice-breaker, the *Yermak*, arriving at Kronstadt harbour in 1899. It was built in 1897–98 at the Armstrong dockyard in Newcastle-upon-Tyne on the orders of Admiral Stepan Osipovich Makarov, and named in honour of Yermak Timofeyevich, the Cossack leader who conquered Siberia in the sixteenth century.

Opposite: The Narva Gate marks the city boundary. A wooden arch was first built on this site to the design of Quarenghi in 1814, to commemorate the heroism of the Russian Guards in the 'Patriotic War of the Fatherland' against Napoleon. In 1827 it was decided to replace this arch with one of metal and brick, which was designed by Stasov, but preserved the main elements of the original. Made of brick, riveted in copper, and with copper sculptures the second arch was opened on 17 August 1834. The chariot of Victory surmounting the arch was sculpted by Baron Klodt who was admired for his horses. His four horsemen also adorned the Anichkov Bridge.

Chapter 2

THE PEOPLE

The capital of a great Empire is like a magnet. St. Petersburg attracted not only natives of the two hundred-odd races of Russia's vast territories, but also merchants, technicians, adventurers, artists and architects from all over the world. In the streets, shops and arcades of the city one heard French, the international language of diplomacy and smart society, and German, widely used in the business world and the civil service, as well as Russian, Polish and various local dialects.

The population of St. Petersburg has been described by writers who lived and worked there – often by means of a characterisation of the city's many recognisable 'types'. One such type is Oblomov, from Goncharov's novel of the same name. Oblomov has grown up on a sleepy country estate but come to Petersburg to take a job in an office. He is presented as the embodiment of sloth, unlike his friend Stoltz, the efficient German. He is a product of the quiet tempo of old Russian country life in the era before the liberation of the serfs and the onset of industrialisation. Ill-equipped for his role as clerk in the stultifyingly bureaucratic system, Oblomov dispatches an important paper to altogether the wrong destination, panics and resigns. Thereafter, despite the encouragement of his German friend, he seldom leaves his lodgings; the difference between the two highlights the way in which Teutonic virtue is supposed to revitalise the lazy Slav. Nevertheless it is clear his creator prefers Oblomov to Stoltz. Oblomov ends his days in the Vyborg suburb of the city where the flocks of chickens and the kitchen gardens recreate something of the country life that, right up until the First World War, continued to exist on the outskirts of the city, importing many of its peasant customs into the capital. Even in the photographs taken at the turn of the twentieth century, we catch a flavour of this world in the images of a carter and his horse, of marriage-brokers plying their trade, and of the peasant girls who brought milk, eggs and vegetables to sell in the city.

In the writings of Gogol we frequently encounter the Petersburg landscape as a background to his characters. To Gogol, Petersburg was 'the graveyard of dreams', and in his nightmarish recreations of the city's vast, empty spaces, he conjures up a world simultaneously claustrophobic and barren. In his story *The Greatcoat*, in the character of Akaky Akakievich, the downtrodden, pen-pushing clerk, he describes with compassion a distinct type of the capital – a city of clerks and foreigners – and in doing so provides a whole series of vignettes – 'the fading of the grey St. Petersburg sky, the northern frost when the streets are filled with civil service clerks hurrying to work . . . a frost so biting that the poor fellows don't know what to do with their noses . . .' He also describes the clerk's living conditions: a flat on the third or fourth floor of some house, two tiny rooms with a passage and a kitchen furnished with a pretension to modern taste where he and his friends would sip tea, munch cheap biscuits, smoke long pipes and hear the old story of how the horse on Falconet's monument had had its tail cropped, and the better part of town where the streets are brighter and livelier, 'where among the pedestrians are pretty, well-dressed women and men with beaver collars, and varnished sleighs fly over the snow, their drivers with red velvet caps and bearskins'.

Writing thirty years after Goncharov's relaxed, almost rural image, and forty after Gogol, Dostoyevsky powerfully evokes the tenements, dank courtyards and meaner streets of the city. Drawing from his own experiences living at the 'Place of the Four Corners', a junction in one of the poor areas of Petersburg, he creates heroes who enact their dramas in buildings crammed with the poor, where it is possible to rent even the tiniest corner of a communal room. In *Crime and Punishment*, Raskolnikov lives out a moral tragedy against this background, and in some of the photographs here we can glimpse the arches and courtyards of this much darker world. Dostoyevsky is often seen as the only writer who foresaw, not only the shadow of the Revolution, but also its outcome: that if a cataclysm were to occur, the future would be completely different from the way in which its protagonists conceived it.

The Russian peasant has a saying, 'God is high in heaven, the Tsar is far away'. In St. Petersburg, however, the Tsar's presence was integral to the life of the city. Not only was there an army of people working to sustain the government, the court, the offices, academies and theatres, all of which fell under direct Imperial control or patronage, but the court ritual and ceremony that attended every move of his public life gave prestige to the capital and touched and directed the lives of its citizens. In contrast to this official role was his more specifically Russian and homely identity as the father of his people. While it lasted the Russian Empire remained essentially a traditional and patriarchal society in which the familiarity that existed between people was evident even in forms of address – for example, the way in which peasants and workmen referred to one another as brother, father, uncle and so on. The Tsar stood at the head of this universal family hierarchy, and the title '*batushka*' by which he was often addressed (of which the English rendering, 'little father', gives only a weak and sentimental reflection) respectfully indicated this position. He was seen as being involved with his people on a personal level – a role best demonstrated by the example of Nicholas I, who acted as censor to the work of Pushkin and who, after the revolt of the Decembrists, rather than turning the conspirators over to be dealt with by the system, instead talked with them and acted as their father-confessor. The story that, on seeing a pauper's coffin going unattended to its burial, Nicholas dismounted from his horse and followed it himself, may well be apocryphal, but is one among many which shows the perceived role of the Tsar. The Tsar's third identity, that of private individual, reflected within the Imperial palaces by the division between state rooms and private apartments, was quite separate from either of the public roles – in engravings and, later, the photographs shown here, the images of public appearances show the Tsar as his subjects glimpsed him; in the picture of the Imperial couple taking a photography lesson, we are seeing a private life that was, especially for Nicholas II, very private indeed.

Apart from the various Imperial palaces occupied by the Great Court, there were also a number of Grand Ducal courts attached to residences in the

Previous page: Selling *sbiten* (a drink made of honey and mixed spices served warm), meat and cabbage pies and gingerbread on the Field of Mars. In the background is the Marble Palace, built by Rinaldi between 1768 and 1785 for Prince Grigorii Orlov, Catherine's favourite, who, with his brother, engineered the coup which brought her to the throne. At the time of its design, the first marble was being quarried in quantities in the Urals and Siberia and the architect made full use of its availability in contrast to the simple stucco façades of most buildings in the capital. Carved on its façade are the words 'In grateful friendship.' In 1782 the palace was bought back from Orlov's heirs, and when Catherine's son, Paul, came to the throne it was put at the disposal of Stanislaus Poniatovsky, the King of Poland, a lover of Catherine before she acceded. In the second part of the nineteenth century it became the home of the Grand Duke Konstantin Nikolaievich, brother of Alexander II.

city belonging to the grand Dukes, the sons and grandsons of the Tsar. They mostly pursued military careers, but their primary function was to give support to the Tsar in his Imperial role. This function was not always punctiliously carried out, but many of the Grand Ducal families supported the arts and literature and contributed much to the glamour of the city.

When Peter the Great founded his new capital he commanded about 350 of the noble families, mainly based in Moscow or living on their estates around the country, to build houses there. Most of these families still had town houses in Petersburg at the beginning of the twentieth century. While the industrial tycoons who played such an important part in the life of the Empire do not enter our story because their activities were primarily based in Moscow, the great noble families' lives and duties revolved very much more around the court. They could mostly date their connections back at least as far as Catherine the Great, and many to the old Russian dynasty of Rurik: they were the most exclusive members of the Russian nobility which, because every court servant was entitled, by the service he rendered, to an hereditary rank – even the lowest rank of the army, that of ensign, conferring nobility – was enormous. Their names occur repeatedly in the captions to the photographs –Dolgorukys, Obolenskys, Yusupovs, Shuvalovs, Stroganovs, Sheremetievs, Kleinmichels and, finally, the Galitzines, an enormous clan numbering over three hundred. On the eve of the First World War, pictures show one of the famous fancy-dress balls at the house of Elisaveta 'Betsy' Shuvalova, whom an English diarist describes as 'the most energetic and forthright lady of her time'. The same social season saw the party hosted by Countess Kleinmichel for her three nieces at which, she boasted, four times as many people as her house could have accommodated were begging her for invitations. Those lucky enough to attend saw, among other things, an Oriental Quadrille costumed by Bakst and led by the grand Duchess Kyril. No wonder guests were fighting for standing room on the stairs.

More peripheral to the life of the town, but with their own special place in Petersburg as in Moscow, were the gypsies. They lived in encampments on the islands, and fashionable restaurants like the *Medved* offered an impressive choir of gypsies to entertain diners with their songs, some plaintive and sad, others savagely intoxicating. Fabergé even made a hardstone figurine of a noted gypsy singer, Vara Panina, whose physical ugliness contrasted with the great beauty of her voice. The manner of her death was dramatic – she took poison while singing a song of unrequited love before an audience which contained its object – an officer of the Imperial Guard. A popular winter pastime was a visit to the gypsy encampments. Parties would set off, wrapped in furs and seated in large sledges, to eat supper at Krestovsky Restaurant on the island of the same name and to enjoy the songs and the dancing of the gypsies in their heavily ornamented and brightly coloured costumes.

Memoirs deal with the lives of the great, and novels with those of the ordinary people. In the same way we have portraits of the famous and genre paintings of everyone else. Photography allows us to hold up a mirror to the past and to bring it to life. Details that were probably too familiar to be noticed at the time can be picked out in these pictures. Often it is the minutiae that strike one most strongly. Picking out faces in a crowded photograph a single direct stare, then fixed on the photographer, now catches the reader with a startling freshness.

Right: A soup kitchen for the unemployed. The meal, eaten from communal bowls, seems to be *kasha*, the traditional Russian buckwheat porridge.

Sleeping quarters at one of the doss houses of the city. No bedding is provided, the men sleeping in shallow wooden compartments like shelves. Rules included the removal of boots indoors.

A group of *izvoshniki* (cabmen). A characteristic sight of the city, their uniform consisted of a heavily wadded sapphire-blue coat with a coloured belt and, generally, a flat beaver hat with an upturned crown. The wadding was intended not only to keep the driver warm, but also to broaden his back and so afford some shelter for his passengers. In this picture the horses are tethered to rings mounted in the kerbstones, still found in many places today. Many street corners were equipped with public mangers where hay was sold in bundles large enough to feed just one or two horses.

A cabman on Nevsky Prospekt, against the background of the garden pavilion of the Anichkov Palace. In addition to his padded coat, his knees are covered by a leather apron, and the cab has a hood to protect the passengers from snow and wet. Many contemporary writers have left accounts of the *izvoshniki*; Augustus Hare, writing in the late nineteenth century, recounts, 'A pedestrian shouts out, "Davai izvoshnik" to the first of the 17,000 *droshkies* which are to be met with everywhere with drivers in kaftans down to their feet who look, as Princess Dashkoff says, as if they had a Turk for their father and a Quaker for their mother. A crowd respond to the call, each driver settling himself as if certain of being the one selected; "Where to, little father? To the Fortress? I'll take you for a rouble." . . . If you take the cheapest, a general jeer arises . . . but no-one enjoys the joke more than the successful candidate, who gathers up his reins and drives off in high humour.'

At about the same time, Kohl writes 'In every street arrangements have been made for the convenience of the *izvoshniks*. There are mangers and convenient descents to the canals or the river. To still the thirst and hunger of the charioteers themselves there are peripatetic dealers in *kvas* and tea who constantly wander the streets. The Russian coachman seems to trust more to the persuasiveness of his own eloquence than anything else. He rarely uses his whip . . . seldom giving (his horse) harder words than, "My brother, my friend, my little father . . . come, pretty pigeon, make use of your legs." '

On the eve of the First World War, Meriel Buchanan, the daughter of the British ambassador, describes the Embassy coachman: 'Like all Russian coachmen, Ivan cultivated a certain stoutness in his long sapphire-blue coat shaped rather like a dressing-gown and tied around the waist with a gold belt . . . In winter (he) wore a blue velvet three-cornered cap with gold braid, and in summer a queer little top hat that was low and squat and had a curled-up brim. He also had three broad gold stripes down his back, the insignia of an ambassador's coachman, a minister's having two stripes and a secretary's only one . . . He never seemed to mind how long one kept him waiting, but would sit for hours in cold or heat, rain or snow, sometimes fast asleep, and sometimes smoking a short clay pipe.'

A small, local market serving the staff of the factory seen in the background.

Marriage-brokers, whose job was to negotiate marriage settlements and fix dowries. By the turn of the century marriage-broking was rarer, but the custom persisted with the peasantry. Brokers traditionally wore a knot of ribbon on the shoulder. Many inhabitants of St. Petersburg had moved in from villages in the surrounding area bringing their country ways with them.

Opposite: A blind street musician, carrying a hurdy-gurdy, led by a boy, soliciting alms. His hat, of uncured sheepskin, indicates that he is probably a 'Little Russian'. The boy wears the more typical 'Great Russian' hat with earflaps.

Queue at a free dining room. Organised by various charitable societies, there were eight of these in St. Petersburg at the beginning of the century.

The unemployed queuing at a labour exchange.

Previous page: Victims of fire, their possessions piled in the street.

Waiting for admission to one of the city's doss houses. The notice reads, 'Don't drink unboiled water. Opens 7p.m. Show passport. Drunks not admitted.' A similar establishment at 13 Maliy Bolotniy Street charged five kopeks for a night's stay, which covered a meal of bread and beef soup in the evening as well as bread and a mug of tea in the morning.

Employees at a warehouse for wine storage. A simple meal of bread and tea was provided at midday. Men and women are segregated. The large, white-tiled stove in the far corner heats the room.

Factory staff enjoying an *al fresco* meal on a works outing.

Opposite: A carter feeding his horse on the outskirts of the city. This picture could have been taken almost anywhere in provincial Russia at the turn of the century.

Quarrying limestone outside the city. The stone was widely used in Petersburg while limewash, one of its products, was used for the exteriors of buildings. The miners did not use explosives, but sank shafts, lined them with wood and flooded them. As the wood expanded, the stone split, enabling layers to be lifted out of the shaft.

Stonebreakers near Senate Square breaking up rubble to be used as a base in roadmaking. Their feet are protected by thick wrappings of rags.

Above left: Studio photograph of a newspaper vendor selling the paper *Ogonyok*.

Above right: A soldier of the Caucasian regiment in dress uniform of armour and chain mail. Alexander Benois describes witnessing their antics in May parades of his childhood: 'The apotheosis of military splendour . . . took place on the vast Tsaritsin meadow . . . the peak of the spectacle was the trick riding of the Caucasian soldiers, the Tcherkess . . . Some of them were still dressed in silver armour, just like medieval knights . . . The trick riders dashed past, some standing on their saddles, shooting backwards and forwards; and when they approached the Imperial tent, they slipped under the bellies of their horses and with incredible nimbleness caught the kerchiefs thrown to them by the Empress or the Grand Duchesses.'

A *stranik*, or wandering pilgrim. Innumerable such figures travelled between the great monasteries and the holy shrines, relying on the charity of those they met. The ultimate pilgrimage was that to Jerusalem by way of Mount Athos. This man, Ivan Petrovich Parfenov, had wandered about Russia for twenty-eight years at the time this photograph was taken.

A carpenter with the tools of his trade.

Above right: A *nyanya*, or wet-nurse, traditionally wore Russian folk costume. Baedeker describes them, 'dressed in bright and rich national costume (blue, when their charges are boys, and pink for girls) ... [They] are a conspicuous feature [of the city]. They generally wear a white mantle richly ornamented with silver tassels; their becoming headgear (*kokoshnik*) is of the same colour, shaped like a diadem and adorned with imitation pearls and silver.' This early photograph shows its subject more simply dressed, but with the traditional dress and *kokoshnik*.

Circus performers, posed with some of their props. Circuses, offering a wide variety of acts, were popular entertainments. The best known was the Ciniselli Circus, located alongside the Fontanka Canal. The two women here strike a note of *fin-de-siècle* exoticism, in keeping with the high standard of costuming of the contemporary stage.

Left: A plumber and his family. A studio photograph, taken in about 1900.

A clerk and his family.

A monk: monasteries were the repositories of a spiritual inheritance which could be traced back to its birthplace in the Egyptian desert. Monks were held in great veneration by the people as the holiest aspect of Orthodox consciousness. The monk's long hair and beard became standard from the period of the fall of Constantinople.

The *dvornik* or yardman of 54 Nevsky Prospekt, shown in a posed genre photograph exchanging eggs and Easter greetings with a peasant girl. The medallion is the badge of his office. The word *dvornik* comes from the Russian *dvor*, or yard. Baedeker remarks, 'They combine the functions of the French concierge, the American choreman, the English hall-porter, and a subordinate police official.'

A peasant in his greasy sheepskins, lounging by a samovar, is a standard image of the rural Russian way of life, which also infiltrated the cities.

Above right: A milkmaid.

A nun.

A baker's boy.

A boy selling matches.

A boy selling abacuses.

Alexander in his study in the Winter Palace. He had occupied the room as Tsarevich, but the Biedermeier style of the room shown in watercolours of the 1830s has given way to a fashionable clutter by the time this photograph was taken in about 1880. A simple camp bed on which the Tsar slept is concealed behind the alcove, and here he was brought to die. After his death the room was shut up and closely guarded by an aged retainer – linen handkerchiefs were still piled on his desk in the way he liked, and even the bloodstained sheets remained on the bed.

Prince Alexander Gorchakov (1798–1883). As a child, he had been the playfellow of Pushkin; he attended the coronation of George IV of England, and conversed with Walter Scott. He was foreign minister during the decade following the humiliation of the Crimean War and, excepting Bismark, he was probably the strongest personality in the chancellories of Europe. His fame in Russia relates to the time when, as an elderly man with a venerable appearance, he studiedly adhered to the style of dress current in his youth.

Opposite: Alexander II, 1855–81, the Tsar-Liberator, among whose first acts on his accession was the ending of the Crimean War. He inherited an Empire which was militarily defeated, diplomatically isolated and socially backward, and was responsible for the transformation of the Empire through a series of major reforms of which the most far-reaching was the liberation of the serfs in 1861. What took a civil war in America was achieved in Russia, despite strong opposition, through Imperial initiative. During his reign Russia underwent rapid industrialisation, but reform and renewal did not create a Utopia and the radical intelligentsia became disenchanted. A fanatical group of terrorists dedicated themselves to a campaign to hunt down and kill the Tsar. The first attempt took place in the Summer Garden, where he habitually walked, but a bystander knocked the pistol out of the assassin's hand. On 1 March 1881, the Tsar was returning from a military review and a visit to his aunt, Yelena Pavlovna, when a terrorist hurled a bomb. He escaped harm, but a number of the Cossack escort and some bystanders were killed and wounded. Alexander insisted on concerning himself with the victims. 'Are you hurt, Sir?' asked a voice from the crowd. 'No, thank God', he replied. 'It is too early to thank God' called another voice, and a second bomb exploded which shattered the Tsar's legs, mortally wounding him. He was driven home to the Palace to die.

Grand Duke Paul, youngest son of Alexander II (1860–1919). Countess Kleinmichel, a well-known leader of society, sentimentally records in her memoirs, 'It was at Nice that I saw the Grand Duke Paul for the first time. He was then a delightful child, five or six years old. My parents and I had been invited to visit the Empress Marie Alexandrovna [consort of Alexander II] at the Villa Bermont, where the Tsarevich had died in the same year . . . The little grand duke came in after dinner. He looked so sweet in his Russian smock of white silk and his little boots with red revers, that I longed to kiss him, but dare not. The Tsaritsa seemed to guess my thought, for she said, "See how my little puss-in-boots stares at you, you must kiss him." I reddened with pleasure at the permission . . .' Paul Alexandrovich was shot in the Peter Paul Fortress in 1919.

Below left: Grand Duchess Maria Nikolaevna, daughter of Nicholas I. She married the Duke of Leuchtenburg, who settled in Russia. Their palace, built by Stackenschneider, stands behind the monument to Nicholas I on St. Isaac's Square. Later it housed the Council of the Empire, Russia's Council of Ministers.

Below right: Maria Alexandrovna, only surviving daughter of Alexander II, who adored her. She married, despite the fervid opposition of the Russophobe Queen Victoria, the latter's son, Alfred, Duke of Edinburgh. It was said that the Grand Duchess's governess, Countess Tolstoy, a nagging perfectionist, was responsible for the look of discontent that was increasingly remarked by all who saw her. She did not adapt successfully to life in England, which she found drab after the glamour of St. Petersburg, and her interests were too intellectual to endear her to the philistine British aristocracy. In later life she became known for her arrogance and her eccentricities, among the latter her insistence on having shoes that were interchangeable, rather than tailored to her right and left feet.

The main staircase of the Michael Palace, home of Grand Duke Michael and Grand Duchess Yelena. The palace is a landmark of the city and a masterpiece of the architect Rossi. After the death of Grand Duke Michael's daughter, Catherine, the palace was acquired by Nicholas II to house the long-planned Museum of Russian Art, named after Alexander III.

Grand Duchess Yelena Pavlovna, wife of Grand Duke Michael and favourite aunt of Alexander II, was an outstanding figure in Petersburg society throughout much of the nineteenth century. She is described in the diary of Kisselev in 1861 as 'a woman of great intelligence with a heart of gold'. Married when very young, she continued to study and kept in touch with visiting scholars: 'she never chatters: she talks. Everyone who has met her marvels at the extent of her knowledge ... Her court is magnificent, her dinners and evening parties exquisite. She does not choose her guests from the upper social layer, her invitations being dictated by a recognition of personal qualities ... her liberal gestures produce little storms in society.' Her charities included children's schools, widows' almhouses and nursing homes and, devoted to music, she played a key role in the founding of the first conservatoire. She exerted a strong influence over Alexander II who, in his liberation of the serfs, depended very much on her support.

Alexander III, 1881–94, ascended the throne during a time of general uncertainty but instantly assumed command of the situation. His first proclamation upheld his conviction in strong leadership as a means of achieving stability. The terrorists had lost any remnants of public sympathy and their organisation was decimated. Alexander appointed a series of trusted ministers to overhaul the country's finances, promote peace in Europe and lay the foundations for industrial development. A gentle giant who resembled a *bogatyr*, his presence inspired awe and respect, and his scrupulous honesty and hard work was not denied by his worst detractors. He simplified the court rituals, introduced military uniforms more on the model of peasant dress and reinforced the cultural inheritance of his Empire at the expense of German influence. By the time of his early death he had laid the basis for a strong Russia. His consort, Maria Feodorovna (1847–1928) was a princess of the small, provincial court of Denmark and a sister of Queen Alexandra of Britain and of King George I of Greece. Diminutive and lively, a good judge of character and with a strong sense of fun, she believed that her chief function was to charm those with whom she came into contact, and over the years made herself universally liked. Here, the Imperial couple are seen with their children: the future Nicholas II, George, who later died of tuberculosis, Xenia, Olga and Michael.

Father John of Kronstadt, 1828–1908, was an outstanding example from a group of Russian Christians possessed of a charismatic and prophetic gift. A dean of St. Andrew's Cathedral at Kronstadt, the chief naval base of the capital, he was admired both as a preacher and a healer. Crowds flocked to him for guidance and help, recognising his unusual powers, and Alexander III called him to his deathbed.

The funeral of Alexander III. He died at his estate at Livadia, in the Crimea, but his body was brought back to St. Petersburg for burial.

Maria Feodorovna, the first picture taken in about 1860, wearing traditional Russian dress, the second in court dress.

Maria Feodorovna in old age. An informal shot, taken by her daugher in the park at her country residence, Gatchina.

The Empress Maria Feodorovna and her first child, the Tsarevich Nicholas Alexandrovich.

Grand Duke Vladimir Alexandrovich, brother of Alexander III (1847–1907). Handsome and imperious, with a ruddy complexion and a voice which carried to the furthest corner of his club, the Grand Duke was a great hunter and a gourmet who kept a collection of menus with his own annotations. A lover of literature and the arts, he was President of the Imperial Academy. Repin's famous painting of the Volga boatmen hung in his palace, built in Renaissance style just a few blocks from the Winter Palace.

Grand Duchess Maria Pavlovna (above), a princess of Mecklenburg-Schwerin, the formidable wife of Grand Duke Vladimir and a key figure in the life of the capital. Strong-minded and professional, fully aware of the duties that attached to her position, she presided over a court the importance of which was accentuated because of the seclusion of the Imperial Great court. On the right she is seen in her drawing-room at the Vladimir Palace. Her surroundings have a *fin-de-siècle* comfort, with chintz-covered sofas and a profusion of palms. The tiara she wears was smuggled out of Russia by an admirer, an English diplomat, and now belongs to the British Crown.

Count Friederickes was an ideal courtier and intimate friend of Nicholas II, who appreciated his simplicity, tact and integrity. A man of charm, he was universally popular. He officially reported to the Tsar twice a week, but when the Imperial family was at Tsarskoye Selo he received an invitation for lunch, a reception or a revue every couple of days. It was to him that Nicholas confided his difficulties in dealing with ministers and Grand Dukes. While the Tsar agonised over the question of his abdication in 1914, Friederickes strongly advised him against giving up the throne, predicting that it would solve nothing but would lead to 'rivers of blood'.

Princess Sophia Sergeevna Shcherbatova (1879–1927). This portrait epitomises the cool elegance of an aristocratic beauty on the eve of the First World War.

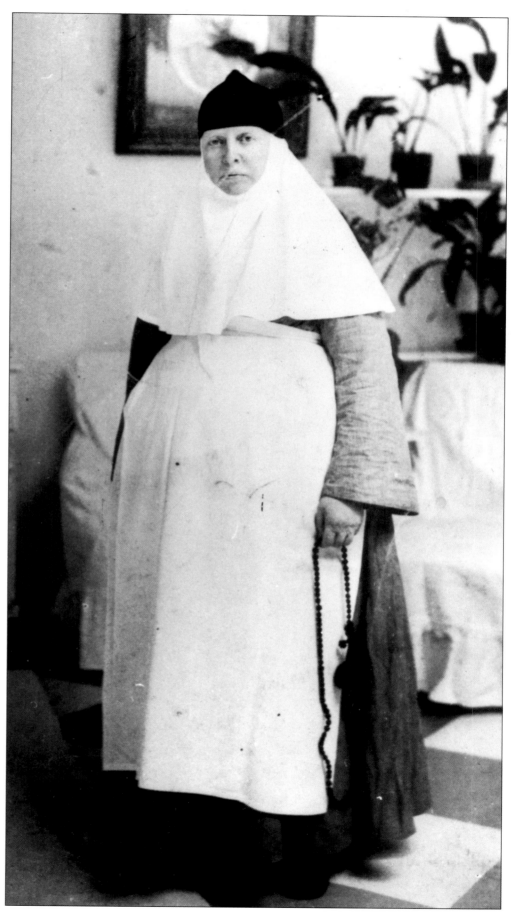

Grand Duchess Alexandra Petrovna, a princess of Oldenburg, married to Nikolai Nikolaevich, a son of Nicholas I, and mother of Nikolai Nikolaevich the Younger (see page 125). Almost all the wives of Emperors and Grand Dukes were from German princely families and most of them embraced Orthodoxy with zeal. Countess Kleinmichel recalls that during the 1860s, when society in Petersburg consisted of only a few families, Alexandra Petrovna was not part of the circle 'for she was entirely given up to religion and received only bishops, priests and monks'. This photograph was taken in about 1890 when the Grand Duchess had altogether assumed a monastic life.

Coachmen and postillions of a court carriage in their distinctive uniform.

The Empress Alexandra Feodorovna and the Tsarevich Alexei Nikolaevich, attending a function during the First World War.

The Empress Alexandra arriving with her two elder daughters for an official engagement. In marked contrast to Maria Feodorovna, the Emperor's mother, Alexandra had no rapport with the public. She was nervous, often ill, and preferred to live a secluded family life. Although dedicated to the country of her adoption she was never popular there. Over the years she became a tragic figure, increasingly isolated even from other members of the Imperial family.

Watching manoeuvres at Krasnoye Selo. The Tsarevich stands at the centre and to his left the Empress is seen sharing an joke with her daughters.

In the Alexandria Park at Peterhof, Nicholas I built himself a modest cottage where he could relax with his family. It was built in the currently fashionable Gothic style by an English architect and was known as the *Kottej*. Here there was a study where he could send signals to his fleet in the Gulf of Finland. He was also accustomed to walk across the park to the large palace of Peterhof to work in the study there. His great-grandson Nicholas II sought seclusion in the same Alexandria Park in a newer villa situated at the edge of the Gulf of Finland. This photograph shows his study there. Among the mementoes on the desk are a Fabergé frame ornamented with an enamelled naval cross of St. Andrew, and a heavy silver-mounted inkwell in the Russian style. The Tsar spent long hours working at his desk on reports, usually retiring here once again after drinking tea in the evening to continue his perusal of documents. When receiving ministers he would listen attentively to their reports and, as a sign that the audience was at an end, stand up, walk to the window and gracefully change the subject.

Right: Nicholas II, his sister Olga and Empress Alexandra Feodorovna during a photography lesson. The family were skilled photographers. A technician was permanently employed to develop their films, the day's photographs being brought for inspection each evening. Pasting photographs into albums was a favourite pastime and scrapbooks lay in profusion about the Imperial family's private apartments.

In 1903 there was a celebrated costume ball to mark the bicentenary of the founding of Petersburg. Curiously, the costume theme chosen was based on the dress of the reign of Tsar Alexis, the father of Peter the Great, called 'the Quiet Tsar', due, no doubt, to the aversion felt by Nicholas II, the Slavophile Tsar, for his august predecessor. Participants at the ball recall the impromptu Russian dance executed on the Tsar's request by the court beauty, Princess Zinaida Yusupova, for which she received rapturous applause. The theme for the ball was a symptom of an increasing fascination with the origins of Russian culture which stimulated an important movement of Russian revivalism in art during the first decade of the twentieth century.

The photographs show the Tsar against a background evocative of the Kremlin's Terem Palace; his sister, the Grand Duchess Xenia Alexandrovna (centre) and Madame Von Larskaya (left). The latter had many of her family jewels adapted to match the costume, and an assistant from Fabergé visited her on the day of the ball to sew the final adornments to her dress. Princess Dolgoruka recalled that the costume suited the Empress and her sister Elizabeth to perfection, while the ballerina Karsavina described the Tsaritsa as 'an icon of rigid beauty'. The Emperor wore a red velvet brocade costume which had belonged to Tsar Alexis. Several other original costumes had been copied for clients by the Moscow dressmaker Lomanova, whose work could not be equalled even by the French couture houses. Twenty-four young couples were chosen to perform a specially choreographed Russian dance for which lessons were given by the ballet master Aistov.

Opposite: Princess Zinaida Nikolaevna Yusupova, photographed at her palace on the Moika Embankment in 1914. The last representative of a great and wealthy family of Tartar origin, known for their eccentricities and their love of the arts, she was married to Count Felix Sumarokov-Elston, who was allowed to take her name to prevent the family from dying out. Everything about this picture indicates her high rank – furniture, lapdog, furs and languid pose. She stirred up considerable feeling at court against the Imperial family when her husband, appointed Governor of Moscow during the Great War, had to be dismissed because of his outbursts of popular anti-German feeling which caused riots in the old capital. The bitterness which he and his wife felt in consequence and the gossip about dark forces around the throne to which this gave rise, had a part to play in preparing the psychological ground for the February Revolution.

The Chevaliers Guards were founded in 1799 by Paul to act as his personal bodyguard. The most glamorous and prestigious regiment in the army, its members were selected for their height, fair complexions and family connections as much as for their suitability to serve. The breeches of the uniform were made of elkskin and had to be dampened to appear absolutely creaseless.

The two Chevaliers shown are Igor Konstantinovich (top) and Dmitri Pavlovich. Dmitri was the son of the brother of Alexander II, Grand Duke Paul. His mother died in childbirth and his father was exiled after remarrying without Imperial approval so he was brought up by the austere Grand Duke Sergei and Nicholas II took a fatherly interest in him. His participation in the murder of Rasputin came as a bitter shock to the Imperial couple and he was exiled to the Persian front. On account of this he was one of the few members of the Imperial family to survive the Revolution. His cousin Igor was murdered in Siberia in 1918.

View of the private theatre in the Yusupov palace, in which the family performed – on occasion joined by members of the Imperial family.

Prince Felix Feliksovich Yusupov, son of Princess Zinaida. A man of exquisite taste with limitless wealth at his disposal, he lived a charmed life, marrying the Tsar's beautiful niece Irina, which further enhanced his glamour. His brother Nicholas was killed in a duel, leaving him sole heir.

The Prince achieved notoriety through the sensational murder of Rasputin in the cellars of the palace on the Moika. In this photograph, taken in 1910, Felix is shown wearing Russian costume for a fancy-dress ball.

The Yusupov palace, a gift of Catherine the Great to Princess Tatiana Yusupova, dates back to the 1760s, when it was said to be the inspiration of the architect Vallin de la Mothe, who had only just arrived in the capital. During the 1830s alterations were undertaken in a more fashionable remodelling, including a hall with Corinthian columns. Thirty years later a sumptuous new model staircase was constructed. The house also contained a mosaic Moorish room, inspired by the Alhambra.

Opposite: On the left of this picture is Prince Vladimir Nikolaevich Orlov, a descendant of Catherine the Great's favourite of the same name. His father and grandfather had been ambassadors and courtiers. A bon vivant and a gourmet who was appalled by the poor standard of the meals served at court, Orlov was also an enthusiast for motoring and was among the first to import cars to Russia. He was universally known as the Tsar's chauffeur for, having introduced Nicholas to motoring, he would allow no-one else to drive him. He subsequently fell out with the Empress because of his outspoken criticism of Rasputin's presence at Court and of his influence.

He is shown here with his brother-in-law, Prince Belasievsky, in the portico of an unidentified building – perhaps one of the churches in the old Russian style that were built at the beginning of the century.

Anna Alexandrovna Vyrubova (1884–1964), an ineffectual figure who idolised the Empress and was mothered by her, was the daughter of the composer Taneyev and, as an intimate friend of Alexandra Feodorovna, who accompanied her everywhere, had to be provided with an official position at court. Because she lived in such close proximity to the Imperial family and acted as a go-between for the Empress and Rasputin, she assumed a role of some importance.

Grigorii Yefimovich Rasputin (1872–1916), healer and 'Man of God', who lived on Gorokhovaya (Pea) Street, was not originally from St. Petersburg. He was a Siberian, whose specific peasant insights brought him to the attention of the Imperial couple who were in despair over the agonies suffered by the haemophiliac Tsarevich, which only Rasputin was able to alleviate. That the Tsar and Tsaritsa were in search of peasant Russia was symptomatic of the period – after all, Rasputin's peasant blouse was more genuine than that donned by Count Tolstoy.

Rasputin's access to the secluded court raised a storm of speculation and rumour. Supposedly a *starets*, a spiritual elder, he nevertheless lived a life of dissipation but his detractors were not believed by the Imperial couple, especially as those who accused him did not themselves lead blameless lives. He proved enormously useful to the political opposition, who circulated stories to bring discredit on the monarchy. Whatever actual influence he may have had on political events – at any rate, it was always haphazard – what counted was that he was generally believed to be the arbiter of the fate of Russia and also, by many, to be a German agent. His sensational murder fits well into the climate of rumour, slander and myth that paved the way for the onslaught on the monarchy prior to February 1917. The historian Katkov has remarked that the life of Rasputin has been the subject for so much sensational melodrama and baseless speculation, 'if one automatically discarded any publication referring to him as a mad monk it would deal with ninety percent of the trash'.

Opposite: A house party at the villa of the Grand Duke Nikolai Nikolaevich on the outskirts of St. Petersburg in 1898. The Grand Duke, here seen smoking a cigar as he fishes, was a soldier of the old school, fascinated by the minutiae of military life. He was Supreme Commander-in-Chief of the Russian army from 1914 to August 1915 when his dismissal by the Tsar was widely criticised – rather surprisingly, as the Grand Duke's stubborn adherence to old-fashioned methods had previously been equally widely censured. On his left sits his wife, Anastasia, daughter of King Nicholas of Montenegro. She and her sister were prone to intrigue, dabbled in the occult, and were so jealous of their social position and precedence at court that they were jokingly referred to as Scylla and Charybdis. Anastasia was responsible for introducing Rasputin to the Imperial couple, but later turned against him. The figure in uniform on the right is Grand Duke Paul.

A grenadier at his post in 1900, complete with distinctive bearskin. The Golden Company of Grenadiers was founded by Nicholas I in 1827. Only war veterans of distinction served. They mounted a guard of honour on the national monuments as well as the Imperial palaces.

Opposite: A society picnic near the capital in summer 1914.

Grand Duke Michael Alexandrovich, left, seated next to his morganatic wife, the Countess Brassova. The younger brother of Nicholas II, he was of a disarming simplicity and had no interest in politics, preferring to live the quiet life of a country gentleman. He was however thrust into the limelight by his liaison with an ambitious married woman, a kind of Russian Mrs. Simpson. After her divorce they married without the permission of the Emperor, were exiled, but were later allowed to return, whereupon she received the courtesy title of Countess Brassova.

The couple were once more dramatically placed in the limelight during the abdication crisis of February 1917, when Michael declined to receive the onus of the Imperial title in the worsening storm. He was shot by the Bolsheviks in mysterious circumstances in 1918. Brassova lived on in emigration until 1952.

Opposite: Ladies-in-waiting wearing court dress. The basic cut of the costume, a re-working of national dress, as worn by the peasants and which itself reflected romanticised reminiscence of the old Muscovite court, was instigated by Nicholas I, who had a strong interest in old Russian style.

Countess Heiden in court dress. On her left shoulder she wears a diamond cypher of the
Empress against a blue ribbon, the insignia of her office as lady-in-waiting. On formal court
occasions, the ladies of the court were only admitted in 'Russian' dress with trains. A
Russian dress is described in detail in the court calendar. It had to be of white silk and off
the shoulders, weighed down with a long train of red velvet embroidered in gold, the colours
being different for the grand ducal courts. Each lady wore a red velvet *kokoshnik* – a tiara-
shaped headdress – also embroidered with gold and often ornamented with jewels.

127

The Ball of the Coloured Wigs, held at the palace of Countess Yelisaveta – 'Betsy' – Shuvalova on the Fontanka Embankment early in 1914, the last social season before the outbreak of war. Successive generations of Shuvalovs played a role in the life of the city and their guests here include most of the prominent social figures of the time, including Count Orlov, Count Tolstoy, Prince Volkonsky, Prince Gorchakov and Prince Dolgorukov.

In 1914 Countess Kleinmichel gave a memorable fancy-dress ball for her three nieces. The Countess remarked that she 'sent over three hundred invitations . . . my house could not hold a greater number, and as the Russian custom is to give supper at little tables it was as much as my kitchen could undertake . . . Every man or woman who had ever left cards on me thought he or she had a right to an invitation and at least a hundred people asked permission to see the Imperial quadrille from the top of the staircase, which I had to refuse.' Remembering the ball, Meriel Buchanan, daughter of the British ambassador, recalls that the Oriental quadrille, shown below, led by the Grand Duchess Kyril and with costumes designed by Bakst, was such a success that it was repeated on a second evening at the palace of the Grand Duchess's mother-in-law, Maria Pavlovna. Of the dancers numbered, 11, in the centre, is Grand Duchess Kyril; 12, Grand Duke Boris; 14, the American, Princess Cantacuzene, and 28, Count Alexander Shuvalov.

The Procurator of the Holy Synod, Nikolai Raev, in his study. The office of Procurator was a civil post, an appointment made by the Emperor. Known as the 'Tsar's Eye', the incumbent was required to oversee the Synod. The Holy Synod itself was created by Peter the Great to replace the patriarchate that he had abolished. A characteristic interior of the period, as is the rather cluttered drawing-room seen beyond it. Note the early wall-mounted telephone by the desk.

General Count A. F. Trepov, 1862–1926, appointed Governor-General of St. Petersburg during the disturbances of 1905, and subsequently Minister of the Interior.

Opposite below: The Holy Synod of the Russian Orthodox Church. The white headdress is the distinctive mark of a Metropolitan, highest rank in the church hierarchy. Until the time of Peter the Great it was worn only by the Metropolitan of Moscow and the Archbishop of Novgorod, but Peter conferred it on all Metropolitans in an attempt to destroy its unique and venerable significance which dated from the period of Kievian Russia.

Above: The imposing buildings of the Senate and the Holy Synod house the most important administrative bodies of the Empire. Linked by an arch, their various façades overlook Senate Square, Horseguards' Parade and the English Embankment. A building to accommodate the Senate existed on this site from about 1760. During the reign of Alexander I, a competition was held for the design of a new building and the winner who emerged was the gifted Karl Rossi, whose architectural complexes, notably Theatre Street and the palace of Grand Duke Michael, are among the last great masterpieces of neo-classical architecture to leave their stamp on the city. The Senate and Synod buildings were completed in 1834, with the work of a team of sculptors and designers.

Previous page: The brass band of the Firemen's Association, a photograph taken on the Field of Mars by Bulla in 1900. The uniform included the traditional baggy Russian trousers which Alexander had re-introduced at the end of the nineteenth century in an attempt to Russify army uniforms, which had originally been based on the rather buttoned-up Prussian model. The fashion spread to other uniforms.

Firefighting in 1900. The heat of the fire
inside the house has melted the snow of the
fierce Petersburg winter, and this has
re-frozen immediately in the sub-zero
temperatures, to encase the house
completely in ice.

A group of fire officers in various uniforms,
photographed in 1903.

St. Petersburg fire brigade during training exercises.

Opposite: A display window mounted by Karl Bulla, the most famous photographer of the city. A wide selection of photographs is shown, including some English and American magazine covers. On the left of the picture are a number of photographs from the front – the photograph was taken in 1904, when Russia was at war with Japan. The notice under the war pictures reads 'Photographs from the Theatre of War.'

The well-established offices of the *Agricultural News*, which included general news as well as farming news and stock prices. Note the icon hung high on the wall on the extreme right in the upper picture and the abacuses – still in use all over Russia even today – and the modern Remington typewriter in the lower one.

Opposite: The editor of the *Petersburg City Council News*.

News vendors waiting for the late edition of the *Stock Exchange Gazette*, a sort of Russian equivalent to the *Wall Street Journal* or the *Financial Times*.

Motorised tricycles setting out to deliver the latest edition. The name of the paper's editor – Propper – and his address on Nevsky Prospekt are painted on the front.

Igor Ivanovich Sigorsky, 1889–1972, one of the great pioneers of aviation. Born in Kiev, he studied aerodynamics in France, but returned to Russia in 1910 and began to build to his own designs. Based in St. Petersburg, he lectured at the Officers' Aviation School, the Polytechnic Institute and the Russian Society of Engineers. In 1912 he became the chief designer of the aviation department of the Russian-Baltic plant. Here he designed several planes, among them the 'Ilia Muromets', named after the peasant's son and his flying horse of Russian folklore. As a pilot he set a number of world records. In 1919 he emigrated to the United States, where he founded his own firm.

Photographers snapping bathers in the Gulf of Finland, just outside the city.

Wind-sailing on the frozen Neva. The sail advertises Nansen's store where all kinds of skiing equipment may be bought.

Launching a helium-filled balloon from the
Petersburg gas works. Its purpose is not
known, but it may have been used as a
means of advertising.

ГРОЗА ЖИЗНИ

ГОГЕЛЬ МОГЕЛЬ
и ЧОРТА БАБУШКА

The Parisiana cinema – as elsewhere in Europe, foreign names were considered smart, and French names particularly chic. Film-going was a popular entertainment; among the films advertised is 'The Storm of Life' – probably an American import. The commissionaire's slightly eccentric uniform reflects a desire on the part of the management to be different in a city that was full of uniforms.

147

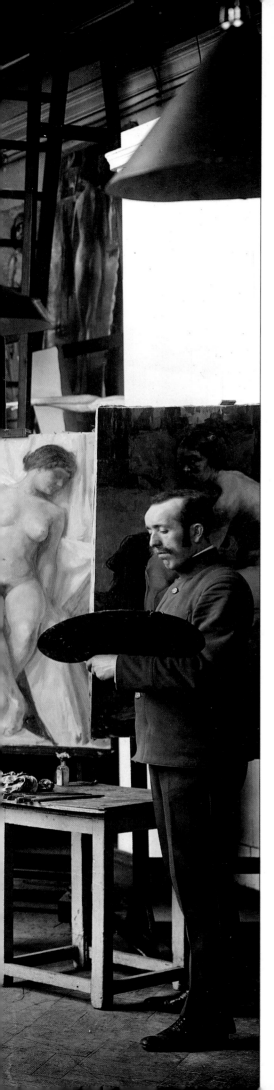

Chapter 3

THE ARTS

Along with adventurers seeking their fortune, artists, architects and writers also converged on St. Petersburg from far and wide. Under Peter's daughter Elizabeth the pragmatic regime was gradually replaced by an atmosphere more auspicious for art. The architect she most relied upon to realise her vision, the Italian, Rastrelli, provided a model of the acknowledged European aesthetic canon of taste then in vogue – the Rococo. Yet there is also something indefinably Russian in his work in the Venice of the North – the result of his encounter with the vastness of the landscape, the scale of the mighty river and the pale northern light. Such impressions evoked a creative response which caused him to build in a style quite distinct from anything he might have produced in his native Italy. Rastrelli was not alone among foreign architects who, largely unknown in their own countries, came to St. Petersburg where they found generous patrons for whom they produced masterpieces.

The European painters who worked in Russia were much less remarkable than the architects. It is therefore surprising that indigenous Russian painting developed so fast and how quickly these minor Europeans schooled a crop of talented pupils. Only the inherent genius of Russian painters can explain the speed with which such artists as Borovikovsky and Levitsky were able to stand comparison with their European counterparts. The Imperial Academy – its exacting teaching and its growing accumulation of art – played a central role in the development of Russian architecture and painting. Founded during the reign of Elizabeth, it was reorganised, expanded and rehoused by Catherine. Students who showed talent were given extensive training and those who won gold medals were automatically despatched abroad to familiarise themselves with the European cultural milieu. Throughout the eighteenth and the first part of the nineteenth century, artistic patronage was primarily in the hands of the monarch.

The selection of architects to construct the Imperial palaces provides an insight into the tastes and characters of successive sovereigns, and likewise to the shift of fashion. It is because the neo-classic style favoured by Catherine initiated a taste which was shared by her successors until the death of her grandson Nicholas I in 1855 that the landscape of Petersburg presents such a unified and harmonious whole. It is probably the greatest European monument to neo-classicism. Catherine's passion for collecting paintings by European masters, which were assiduously pursued by her agents abroad, was imitated by those wealthy enough to do so, as is evidenced by the picture galleries assembled by the Stroganovs, the Yusupovs and others. Such an accumulation of art always reflects a growth of confidence and wealth; the Russian star was rising.

The personality of Nicholas I left its stamp on Petersburg in many ways. The last great builder, who scrupulously oversaw plans for the city, he also founded and endowed the Imperial theatres. His reign saw the fullest development of the formal classical ballet, traditionally an art of the court, in which Italian dancers were attracted to perform. From this there grew and spread a Russian fascination with dance and with the technique and rigorous training that by the beginning of the twentieth century made the Russian ballet the best in the world. During Nicholas's reign, which also coincided with the golden age of Russian literature, the great Romantic painter was Briullov, whose colossal masterpiece, 'The Last Day of Pompeii' elicited the admiration of Walter Scott and won the Paris Grand Prix of 1834, thereby putting the French master Ingres in the shade. Such recognition on the part of the West was important to Russia, and some of her critics hailed 'The Last Day of Pompeii' as 'the first day of Russian art'.

After the death of Nicholas in 1855 Russia underwent far-reaching changes. In the sphere of art a new social group, the intelligentsia, usurped the function of the monarch in setting fashionable trends. The starting point of their world view was a cult of the peasant, to whom they ascribed greater moral stature than people at other levels of society, and they believed that by undermining social injustice they could ensure his future awakening. The intelligentsia emphasised tragic events and grim moral issues. Although guided by atheistic materialism, their quest for justice and their preoccupation with what were then called 'accursed questions' – questioning the meaning and purpose of life – could be characterised as an essentially spiritual energy deflected to secular ends. Literature was the main field of their activity and under their influence painting could be seen to assume aspects better suited to writing. Guided by the taste of the intelligentsia the public insisted that art should expound three themes, all derived from literature – that it should have social content, that it should be 'realistic' and that it should be quintessentially Russian. The gathering momentum of neo-Russian revivalism was a logical reaction to an earlier attitude which had regarded anything Russian as synonymous with barbarism.

Ilya Repin is regarded as the greatest artist who subscribed to the ideals of the intelligentsia as they were formulated during the seventies and eighties. At a time when content was more important than technique, so that Yakobi's painting, 'The Prisoners' Resting Place' was praised less for its brushwork than because it was instrumental in securing an alleviation of the conditions under which prisoners were transported, Repin's celebrated canvas 'The Volga Boatmen' won Dostoyevsky's approval when it was first exhibited in 1873. Significantly Dostoyevsky placed the painting in context by comparing the artist with the writer Gogol, commenting that it gained in stature because it did not sacrifice truth to dramatic effect and to arouse moral indignation. The painting was acquired by the President of the Academy, Grand Duke Vladimir. Repin also experimented with historic themes. One such canvas shows Ivan the Terrible mourning over the body of the son whom he has struck down in rage. Repin's stark portrayal of blood gushing from the head wound of the mortally wounded Tsarevich caused ladies to faint when this essay in Russian realism was first exhibited in 1885.

The painting and personality of Repin largely dominated the artistic scene during the latter part of the nineteenth century. The photograph on page

Previous page: A life class at the Imperial Academy of Art. The Academy was established in November 1757 on the initiative of Count Ivan Shuvalov, the brilliant favourite of the Empress Elizabeth. Under Catherine the Great it was reorganised and a school for children from the age of six was set up there. The complete course was fifteen years long, beginning with simple copying work, and moving on to life classes, then, in the senior classes, working in a single specialisation: architecture, sculpture, or historical or portrait painting.

Before graduating pupils had to work on specific projects, and for these gold or silver medals of different grades were awarded. The gold medallists were sent to study abroad.

The Academy housed a number of different collections – galleries of Russian and foreign painting, a court of plaster casts and an important library with a large collection of drawings. The building itself was designed by Vallin de la Mothe and A. F. Kokorin in the 1760s and was completed in 1788.

Until the 1840s, outstanding figures and patrons of Russian culture, such as Count Alexander Stroganov (1733–84), a friend of the Emperor Paul and the head of an ancient family who were prominent and well-established collectors and patrons of the arts, were presidents of the Academy. From the mid-nineteenth century it became traditional for members of the Imperial family to hold the presidency, and Grand Duchess Maria Nikolaevna, Grand Duke Vladimir Alexandrovich, and his widow, Grand Duchess Maria Pavlovna, successively held the office.

179 shows him in his studio with the influential critic Vasilii Stasov, who was responsible for propagating the ideals of his generation. Stasov was as dismissive of Bruillov's 'Last Day of Pompeii' as he was scathing of the new *fin-de-siècle* trends that were emerging. Repin was his ideal painter. In the same photograph, Gorky represents the younger generation. At the end of his life his earlier friendships formed an important link with an older generation of giants who were once again widely perceived as models.

Repin was immensely admired by the general public as well as by the establishment. Every honour was heaped upon him, but it is possible to argue that as a painter he was outclassed by his gifted pupil Valentin Serov. Remembered as a landscape artist with a lightness of touch and a fresh handling of colour characterised by a range of silvery-grey tones, he is also a portrait painter whose canvases provide a complete gallery of the outstanding personalities of his day. Serov, who died in 1911, is a transitional figure between the doctrinaire realism of Repin's generation and a new climate of opinion.

Reaction against the aesthetic values of the 1870s and '80s united a younger generation growing up in the 1890s. Followers of the new trend were known as the World of Art group, a name they acquired from the magazine published by the impressario Diaghilev, and their activities were formulated by Alexander Benois. Rejecting the social and didactic purposes of art, Benois and Diaghilev propagated a new approach under the banner of 'art for art's sake'. Both were engaging personalities characteristic of their period, cosmopolitan, well educated and versatile, in contrast to the more humble and insular backgrounds of the generation they supplanted. Petersburg artists of the World of Art group were labelled as decadent, principally because of the variety and breadth of their knowledge and interests: they knew too much and believed too little. Their art had an almost brittle refinement, their paintings were imbued with historical allusion, nostalgia and poetic symbolism.

These qualities were particularly suited to the theatre. It was with stage design that the World of Art group scored its most resounding success. Having for so long followed in the footsteps of the West, Russia now provided a startling model for the West to copy. Diaghilev, who had already organised an important exhibition of Russian portraiture in the Tauride Palace in 1905, felt passionately about bringing Russia's creative achievement to the notice of the West. He brought the first comprehensive exhibition of Russian art to Paris in 1906. Before this, icons had not been seen abroad. It is a significant indicator of the times that social realist painters of the Wanderers group were largely omitted. But the ballets he brought to Paris and London were his greatest triumph. The disciplined training of the dancers, the rich tradition of folk art and the use of professional artists to design the costumes and sets contributed to a unique synthesis: the West had seen no such riot of brilliant colour or vitality and the audiences were stunned by the exoticism, even barbarism of the Russian stage.

The photographs reproduced here relate to a period when Russian creative drive was becoming even more confident. All traces of an earlier inferiority in comparison with the West were discarded. On the eve of 1914, St. Petersburg ranked alongside Paris in its innovatory arts and its outstanding personalities as one of the great intellectual and cultural centres of Europe.

Marius Petipa for fifty years reigned supreme as chief choreographer of the Imperial Ballet at the Marinsky Theatre, where all the dancers were trained by him in a classical repertoire. He served under three Emperors and staged over sixty ballets. In the time he spent in the capital whence he arrived from France, his productions were sumptuous, with enormous casts and large formal processions interrupting the action, which consisted of a number of virtuouso set pieces. Petipa excelled in organising a great number of dancers into an elegant and coherent sequence. By the beginning of the century, however, his style was outmoded, and his gifted pupil, Tamara Karsavina, permits herself to record that he was more feared than liked and that she personally considered him 'a poor actor and dancer'. She even mimicked him behind his back.

Petipa's celebratory performance at the Marinsky, which marked his fifty years in St. Petersburg, was attended by the entire court and presided over by the Emperor and two Empresses in the Imperial box. There was a great mood of expectation – 'What do you have for us on the agenda today, Mr. Petipa?' asked the Minister of the Court. But the performance was a catastrophic climax to his career. There were catcalls from the gallery, the occupants of the boxes looked displeased, and the loud voice of Grand Duke Vladimir could be heard exclaiming, 'Let's take ourselves off home.'

As a reaction to the classicism of Petipa it was Fokine who invented a more natural and expressive style of dancing which nonetheless benefited from the exacting discipline laboriously inculcated at Petipa's ballet classes. It was with this revitalised Russian ballet that Diaghilev conquered the West.

The ballerina Tamara Platonova Karsavina, one of the great ornaments of the Marinsky stage, who was brought to the West in Diaghilev's Paris Seasons. Her memoirs record the world of the dance with great charm. The encouragement and sympathetic interest of members of the Imperial family, notably Alexander III, his brother Vladimir and Nicholas II is evident: 'On December 6, the Emperor's nameday', writes Karsavina, 'the three Imperial theatres gave a special matinee . . . which was attended by schoolchildren . . . In the interval there were bubbling samovars with tea and fragrant cool almond milk served by staff in red livery embellished by Imperial eagles . . . On one such occasion we were taken to the Imperial box . . . Alexandra Feodorovna, the Empress, and Marie Feodorovna, the Empress Dowager, stood in the drawing-room at the back of the Imperial box and handed us sweets. The Tsar stood by. He asked, "Who is the little girl that danced the golden fish?" and I stepped forward and made a deep curtsey.' The Emperor asked how the maiden's ring was found when swallowed by the fish, and little Karsavina showed the small opening in the papier-mâché fish where the ring was put, explaining how it worked. 'The Tsar smiled, "Thank you for explaining. I would never have guessed." His smile had an irresistible charm . . . to me it was like being lifted to Paradise.'

Mikhail Mikhailovich Fokine (seated, in the foreground) with his family. Fokine was born in St. Petersburg in 1880 and trained with the Imperial Ballet. A great dancer, from 1911 he was one of the stars of Diaghilev's Russian Seasons, and partnered Pavlova, Karsavina and Kchessinska. From 1901 he also taught at the Petersburg Theatre School. He was an innovative choreographer, integrating elements of folk and ethnic dance into classical ballet. For the staging of such ballets as 'Pavillon d'Armide', 'Egyptian Nights', 'Le Spectre de la Rose' and 'Petroushka' he worked in cooperation with some of the most famous artists of the day – Bakst, Benois, Dobuzhinsky, Roerich and Goncharova – and the composers Glazunov, Rachmaninov, Stravinsky and Richard Strauss. After 1918 he worked abroad, first at the Paris Opera and then in New York. He died in 1942.

Fokine as Atslan in the ballet '*Le Dieu Bleu*'.

Above right: The ballerina Agrippina Yakovlevna Vaganova (1879–1951). One of the great attractions of the Marinsky, she was the only star to remain in the city after the Revolution. She became director of the Petrograd State Choreographic School, training a new generation of dancers to the same level of technical excellence as before the Revolution.

Right: Vaganova in the ballet 'Don Quixote'.

Opposite: Matilda Feliksovna Kchessinska, the celebrated prima ballerina of the Marinsky, left, with her brother and sister, in 1900. All three were dancers. Josef Kchessinsky, four years older than Matilda, danced at the Marinsky from 1886 and often partnered his more famous sister. He died during the siege of Leningrad in 1942.

Kchessinska in her white villa at 2/4 Bolshaya Dvoryanskaya, built at the beginning of the twentieth century by Alexander Gogen. Although its exterior has pronounced features of *fin-de-siècle* Art Nouveau it is interesting that the interior furnishings reflect the revival of interest in a cool neo-classic style which is characteristic of many smart Petersburg interiors of the time.

Kchessinska studied at the Imperial Ballet School in Rossi's stately neo-classic Theatre Street until 1890 and was one of the chief attractions of the Marinsky until 1917. Said to have been the mistress of Nicholas II when he was Tsarevich, in emigration she married Grand Duke Andrei Vladimirovich (the third son of Grand Duke Vladimir and Maria Pavlovna, see page 108). Her villa was occupied during the February Revolution by representatives of the Bolshevik party, and Lenin frequently harangued the crowds from Matilda's balcony while she instigated a lawsuit to evict her unwelcome guests.

Opposite: Anna Pavlova in rehearsal at the Marinsky Theatre with her partner Marcel Berge. This picture was taken in the summer of 1914, her last season in St. Petersburg. An outstanding ballerina, she was the daughter of an officer of the prestigious Preobrazhensky Regiment, who died when she was a child, and a laundress. She entered the Imperial Ballet School in 1891 at the age of ten. The school was directly funded by the Imperial court and pupils gave performances twice a week, on Wednesdays and Sundays. She began to perform at the Marinsky in 1899. In 1909 she participated in Diaghilev's first Russian Season in Paris, and by 1910 was touring with her own company to enormous international acclaim.

Anna Pavlova resting after rehearsal. She introduced the first thoroughbred English bulldogs into Russia and with these she was often photographed. When, in 1915, she set up her school of dance in England – in a Hampstead house with a large garden – her interest in pets had expanded. She now kept a menagerie of animals which included gazelles and swans.

Above right: The Marinsky Theatre, the most famous in Petersburg, built on Theatre Square on the order of Alexander II by the architect A. K. Kavos after an earlier structure was destroyed by fire. The name commemorates Alexander's consort, Maria Alexandrovna. The Imperial theatres were built and maintained from the Tsar's privy purse and enjoyed strong Imperial patronage and support. In the right foreground is the monument by the sculptor R. R. Bach to the composer Glinka, remembered for his introduction of Russian folk themes and melodies into more formal compositions, erected in 1906.

The Marinsky season always began with a performance of Glinka's patriotic opera, 'A Life for the Tsar'. The theatre seated 2,000, its rich blue and gold interior arranged in tiers of seats and boxes, centred on the main Imperial box which was surmounted with big golden eagles. Although a large number of the more expensive seats were subscribed by the richer patrons, contemporary accounts concentrate on the critical discernment and extravagant enthusiasm of the audience in 'Paradise', the name assigned to the area of cheaper seats in the gallery.

Right: Anna Pavlova dancing with Vaslav Nijinsky in '*Pavillon d'Armide*' which was first performed at the Marinsky on 25 November 1907. Benois began work on the decor of this ballet in 1901 with Fokine choreographing for the graduation exercises of the Imperial School. In the same year Cherepnin completed the music for the first and third scenes. The production was beset with difficulties. Kchessinska, originally billed to dance Armide, withdrew a few days before the première and Anna Pavlova took her place. Diaghilev brought the production to Paris in May 1909 to launch the first of his Russian Seasons. It was here that Nijinsky made his triumphal debut.

Far right: Anna Pavlova as Sylphida in the ballet 'Shopeniana' in 1907.

Konstantin Andreivich Somov (1869–1939) was a founder member of the World of Art group. Born in St. Petersburg in 1869, the son of an eminent historian and curator of the Hermitage collection, Somov was educated at the noted May College, where his classmates included Alexander Benois, Walter Nuvel and Dimitri Filosov, all of whom joined him in shaping the World of Art movement. Somov progressed to the Imperial Academy and later spent time painting in Paris. A sensitive and talented artist, some of his paintings are sensual and brittle to the point of decadence. He was a book illustrator, portrait painter and landscape artist whose works, in the spirit of the times, are immersed in an aura of the theatrical. Here, Somov is seen in his drawing-room. The oval miniature above the piano is a sketch by Serov.

Mstislav Valerianovich Dobuzhinsky, photographed at home with his wife and family in 1908. Of all the World of Art group, Dobuzhinsky is probably the single artist most identified with the city of St. Petersburg and its architecture. He executed many graphic views of the town and in 1921 was to produce an album of lithographs of its streets and buildings. Like the other members of the group his creative work centred around the theatre and he designed costumes and scenery for the Moscow Arts Theatre and the new Drama Theatre, founded by the actress Vera Komissarzhevskaya.

Opposite: Vera Feodorovna Komissarzhevskaya, a well-known dramatic actress, in her study. Komissarzhevskaya was born in St. Petersburg into an artistic family and made her acting debut at the Alexandrinsky Theatre in 1896. In 1904 she founded her own company, playing leading roles in the plays of Ibsen, Chekhov and Gorky. Her study, with its bamboo desk and shelves, oriental vases and fan and clutter of pictures and ornaments, is typical of an 'artistic' interior of the time.

Provincial actors who appeared in various plays visiting the theatres of the capital. Many of these portraits were sold as postcards.

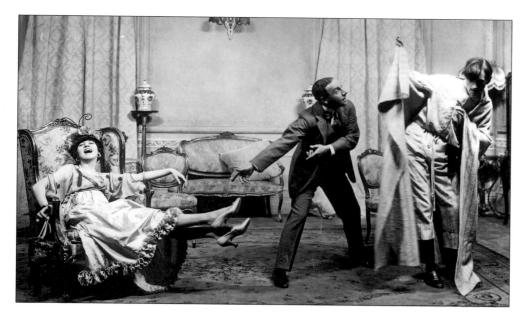

A performance at the Saburov Theatre in the *Passage* (colloquially known as the Passage Theatre) at 48 Nevsky Prospekt. It was situated in the arcade of the great department store, designed by the architect R. A. Zhelyazevich and built in the 1840s, which occupied the whole of the site between Nevsky and Italian Street. The large hall, built on the Italian Street side, was used for plays, lectures and concerts. Between 1904 and 1906 it served as the theatre for Komissarzhevskaya's company. The scene shown here is from the play *Shalaya Babyenka* ('Crazy Woman'), a light comedy.

The actress K. Lenskaya in a pose and style of costume which strongly recall the era of Sarah Bernhardt.

A trio of actresses appearing in a historical play of Russian life at the *Narodniy Dom* (House of the People) Theatre.

The actress Victoria Kadetskaya, simultaneously posing for an artist and the photographer in 1912.

Nicholas Figner, the popular lyric and dramatic tenor, at home with his wife, Renée, in 1911. He sang at the Marinsky Theatre between 1887 and 1907, where he was remembered for his interpretation of the role of Herman in Tchaikovsky's opera, 'The Queen of Spades'. The room is crowded with photographs of his various roles.

Figner with an array of the presents and flowers given to him to mark his thirty years in the theatre, in 1910. Among the opulent gifts some would appear to be Fabergé.

Right: Max Linder, the French actor and music-hall star, posing with cinema owners of St. Petersburg during a promotional visit for his films. One of the most successful actors during the silent era, he enjoyed enormous popularity in Russia.

Opposite: Figner made up for an operatic role, posing backstage with his wife and his daughter, Margarita.

Fyodor Ivanovich Chaliapin, the most renowned singer of his day, in the role of Boris Godonuv, from the opera by Mussorgsky, in 1913. Born in Kazan, Chaliapin performed for the first time in the capital in 1894. He sang almost every major role ever written for a bass, but concentrated chiefly on Russian opera, the works of Mussorgsky, Rimsky-Korsakov and Glinka. In Petersburg he sang at both the People's Opera House and the Marinsky, and in Moscow at the Bolshoi Theatre.

Chaliapin sculpting a self-portrait.

Chaliapin skating with his wife and sisters.

Chaliapin in a group portrait taken at 'Penate', the country house of the artist Ilya Repin (seated second from left, see page 176). Repin painted a much admired portrait of Chaliapin lounging on this sofa, holding a French bulldog, in 1914. This photograph was probably taken in a break between sittings.

Arkady Averchenko, a well-known humour writer, taken in 1913.

Opposite: The writer Leonid Andreyev in 1913. A serious and rather melancholy man, his symbolist plays and sensational works, reflecting the climate of the new era, were admired by, among others, Stasov and Gorky. Maurice Baring, writing in 1910, remarks that 'Andreyev has given us the nightmare of the younger generation.'

Vasily Vasilievich Vereschagin was hugely popular during his lifetime as a painter of battle scenes, and was also one of the Russian painters best known abroad as the result of his travels and exhibitions. Having completed his studies at the Imperial Academy, he worked for a while in the studio of Gérôme in Paris. Vereschagin depicts, not the pomp and circumstance of war, but the suffering and heroism of the individual soldier. In 1868 he organised the Turkestan exhibition where his canvases caused a sensation because the Central Asian campaign was then topical and because of the anti-war nature of his pictures. Alexander II and his consort were seen to gaze long at these works which they subsequently acquired and hung in their private apartments. Vareschagin perished during the Russo-Japanese war of 1904 when the great battleship *Petropavlovsk* sank near Port Arthur.

A cossack and his horse pose for art students in the class of Professor Semionovich-Samokish, a specialist in military themes.

174

Andrei Chukovsky, the universally loved children's writer and critic, posing in front of his portrait in Repin's studio. A painting of Tolstoy rests on the easel.

Years later, when Repin's country dacha was separated from Soviet Russia by the new frontier of independent Finland, Stalin, Russia's new master, who had succeeded in persuading the country's greatest musician, Prokofiev, and the greatest writer, Gorky, to return from emigration, regularly sent Chukovsky as his emissary to persuade the greatest Russian artist to return. Repin never did, but his diaries reveal that he was quite prepared to do so. It was Chukovsky who constantly advised caution. It saddened Repin that the letters he addressed to friends in St. Petersburg were not delivered because he could never bring himself to write 'Leningrad' on the envelopes.

Repin teaching a life class among his pupils at the Academy. An academic naturalistic painter and a member of the *peredvizhniki*, or 'Wanderers', who saw their work as an instrument for social reform, his genre and historic pictures and his portraits enjoyed more fame and admiration than any other artistic work of the time.

The writer Maxim Gorky and the actress Maria Andreeva, posing in the studio at Repin's *dacha*. Gorky was hailed early in his career as a rising star for Russian literature. His early writings are masterpieces full of vivid insights; his later work was taken up by confrontations between stereotyped characters as he struggled to express his revolutionary ideals. A realist, he nonetheless portrayed romantic characters who broke the law and were liars, thieves and murderers while being also sincere, brave and passionate. When, at the outbreak of the Great War, Gorky launched an attack on Dostoyevsky, protesting at the staging of his works in the capital, his antagonism was thought to be a curious survival from the bigotry of the 1870s. In fact it was a foretaste of things to come.

Resting after the sitting. Repin's wife, Natalya Nordman, is
seated on the right, and the bearded figure in the centre of the
picture is Vasily Stasov, a critic whose opinions on art,
architecture and literature dominated the artistic world from
the mid-century to the emergence of the World of Art during
the 1890s. He was a whole-hearted supporter of the Wanderers
and of Repin in particular. In a letter to Stasov in 1872 Repin
wrote, 'Now it is the peasant who counts', reflecting on a
climate in which a new and socially relevant theme was enough
to secure the success of a work.

The composer, Pyotr Ilyich Tchaikovsky. Born in Votkinsky in 1840, he studied law before becoming one of the first students of the St. Petersburg conservatoire in 1862. He taught in Moscow for some years before returning to Petersburg. He was one of the first composers to work with choreographers in writing ballet scores – before this, choreography was looked upon as an entirely separate element which must fit around ballet music, rather than as an integral part of a score. He enjoyed enormous contemporary popularity in Russia, and died in Petersburg in 1893.

Repin working in his study at 'Penate'.

Chapter 4

THE INSTITUTIONS

Imposing public buildings contributed to the aura of majesty that marked Petersburg. The great cathedrals and Imperial residences have already been mentioned, but such an Empire must have a court which is maintained on a scale commensurate with its status and its aspirations to a civilising influence, and such a court requires management. In Petersburg there was a building to house the Imperial archives and another for the administration of the court; the actual machinery of government was housed in various buildings so imposing as to cause the historian Prince Mirsky to refer to 'the sublimation of a military and bureaucratic Empire'. Most striking of these is an architectural complex devised by Rossi to form a semi-circle across a broad square in front of the Winter Palace. This incorporated the Foreign Office, the Ministries of War and of Finance and the Headquarters of the General Staff above an imposing arch topped by a stately bronze Roman chariot with larger-than-life-sized figures. Imperial Rome was evoked elsewhere in further structures of monumental proportions – among them Zakharov's Admiralty and yet another complex by Rossi built to house the Senate and the Holy Synod.

Embassies play an essential part in the life of any capital. Much interesting material on the city and its inhabitants is derived from the memoirs and despatches of ambassadors, who operated from buildings which were necessarily prestigious to reflect the status of their countries. There were also a great number of regimental barracks and their attendant churches and parade grounds in the city, where the pageantry and spectacle of precisely orchestrated reviews was a daily occurrence.

Schools, theatres and museums, many of them Imperial foundations, stood out among the ordinary town houses lining the streets and canals. All these buildings created a theatrical backdrop against which the citizens pursued their daily lives. Reference has already been made to Petersburg types, to the officials, soldiers and foreigners, the artists and the floating character of many who were attracted there. These were actors for whom the stage of Petersburg was set and they had little in common with the people who can be seen today in the city renamed Leningrad.

The first institution of which a child would have experience was school. In 1900 there were 128 secondary schools in the capital, and among these the most exclusive were the Alexander Lyceum and the Smolny Institute (see pages 186–195) – both Imperial foundations. The Alexander Lyceum originated from the desire of the Emperor Alexander I to provide a suitable regime for his younger brothers, Nicholas and Michael Pavlovich, and in the wish of his statesman Speransky to create a forum to prepare boys for positions of responsibility, primarily in government service, diplomacy and the legal professions. Located in a wing adjoining the Imperial Catherine Palace at Tsarskoye Selo, the Lyceum was separated from Alexander's private study only by a long corridor. Pupils were hand-picked and Alexander knew them all by name.

The Smolny Institute, in buildings within the confines of the blue-and-gold convent which Rastrelli had built for Elizabeth, reflected Catherine's concern to promote the education of girls. The photographs of life at the Smolny, taken at the turn of the century, attest to a lifestyle that maintained something of eighteenth-century poise. The artist Levitsky painted some delightfully casual portraits of Smolny girls rehearsing a school play, which Catherine hung in the Peterhof Palace. Against these pictures of demure Russian upper-class girlhood, it is worth remembering that Russian women surprised Western Europeans by the confidence with which they held their own in conversation with men, by the way they smoked openly in public, and by their air of independence, long before such liberated behaviour was acceptable in the West.

For those families intent on their sons pursuing a military career, nothing could compare with the prestige of the Corps des Pages. Sited in a mansion first built by Rastrelli for Elizabeth's vice chancellor and favourite, Vorontsov, the Corps des Pages reared an élite warrior caste. Qualifications for entry were strict; students were expected to be of good family and to have military connections. The names of candidates were put down at birth. Students entered the school at twelve to follow a course of five years of general education and two of specialisation before entering a regiment of the guards. From among the students, boys were chosen to be *Kammerpages* – that is to say, they were attached to the suite of a member of the Imperial family to serve at court functions before returning to their studies.

The May School was one of a number which catered for boys of a less socially elevated background. It was attended by cosmopolitan, upper-middle-class students, many from the intelligentsia. Alexander Benois remembers that he tried to persuade his parents to send him to the Lyceum because he admired the uniform and dreamed of becoming a statesman, but in the end found the May School entirely to his taste, 'no uniform was worn, the majority of my schoolfellows belonged to the middle classes, the school did not open the way to any particularly brilliant careers but I found something much more valuable. I found homeliness ... moderate liberty, warmth between the teaching staff and the pupils and respect for the individual ...' It was while he was at the May School that Benois first began to gather about him like-minded friends with an interest in art, the theatre and history. They called themselves the Nevsky Pickwickians and it was from their ranks that the *fin-de-siècle* art movement known as the World of Art emerged.

The variety of schools in the capital, some Imperial foundations, others church-run or managed by charitable institutions country-wide (the Marie Institute for Girls had its counterpart in every other city in the country) is reflected in the photographs, which convey something of the range of education on offer.

The highest administrative and legislative state institution in Petersburg was the Council of the Empire, which acquired its definitive form during the reign of Alexander I. In its chambers, legislation initiated by ministers was presented for discussion and amendment. In the absence of the Emperor, a

Previous page: A meeting of the directors of the Imperial Academy of Art. Grand Duchess Maria Pavlovna (see page 108), the President, presides at the centre of the picture under an imposing statue of Catherine the Great. She wears mourning for her husband, Grand Duke Vladimir, the previous President, who died in 1907.

chairman of the Council presided over its deliberations. All ministerial appointments were however made by the Emperor himself. A minister could not resign of his own volition – he could only be dismissed. By the beginning of the twentieth century the Council met in the Marinsky Palace opposite St. Isaac's, which had been built for Maria Nikolaevna, eldest daughter of Nicholas I. It was here that Repin's monumental canvas of a session in progress was hung and widely admired.

The Imperial *Duma*, or Russian Parliament, was inaugurated in 1906 as a result of new principles of government formulated by an Imperial manifesto of 7 October 1905. It was an elected national assembly convened to cooperate with the Tsar's ministers in the government of the country. Its sessions were held in Starov's masterpiece, the Tauride Palace, originally built for Catherine's one-eyed statesman and sometime lover, Potyomkin.

Institutions imply uniforms. In 1902 Henry Norman, a visiting British Member of Parliament, was surprised at the number of uniforms to be observed in the streets of the capital, commenting, 'Uniform in fact is the Russian's passion. There are numerous uniformed officers, civil and military generals – nine-tenths of the middle classes wear a uniform – it stamps (the Russian) as a member of the governing class. All this causes confusion to the foreigner who is in danger of exhibiting a railway ticket to a major general or making a deferential bow to a railway guard.'

It was smart in St. Petersburg to belong to a club, of which there were many, catering for specific interests and professions. The Imperial Yacht Club on Morskaya Street was the ultimate in snobbery, with a membership of no more than 150. It had a good chef and elegant premises, and in its congenial atmosphere, where even the Grand Dukes were in the habit of dropping in, friendships were formed and careers made and sometimes destroyed. Many military men used it as a base. Countess Kleinmichel recalls that previously quite ordinary people had a tendency to become unbearable once they gained admittance. There was nothing else quite like it.

The English Club dated from the reign of Catherine and here members played chess and cards and discussed the affairs of the day, while the New Club, as its name implies, was modern and rather dashing. It was founded by the Grand Duke Vladimir and it attracted a membership that was elegant and a little fast. Here there was gambling, good food and witty conversation.

In the number and variety of its museums and institutes Petersburg could hold its own with any European city. Among these were the Academies of Arts and of Sciences, the museums of agriculture, of industrial art, and the private collections of Grand Duke Michael Nikolaevich and of the explorer Simyonov. The star attractions were the Imperial Hermitage and the Alexander III Museum of Russian Art. Admission was for the most part free, for stress was laid on the educational nature of a museum in the lives of ordinary people.

The pictures here suggest something of the range of the city's institutions – those concerned with government, and others which were for education or entertainment.

A harp lesson at the Smolny. Portraits of eminent former pupils hang on the classroom walls.

A pupil of the celebrated Smolny Institute, founded by Catherine the Great who, the most intellectual ruler in Europe, was determined to provide a serious education for the daughters of the nobility. Pupils entered the Institute at six and left at eighteen. The school was located in the Smolny Convent, an extravagantly rococo edifice, reflecting the mid-eighteenth century taste of Elizabeth and built by her favourite architect, Rastrelli. The architectural complex was added to during the first decade of the nineteenth century by the noted architect Quarenghi. Here a schoolgirl is shown dressed in the old-fashioned, distinctive uniform – a plain, fitted dress covered by an apron and a starched linen shoulder cape.

A dance lesson in the main hall. The use of scarves was popularised by the American dancer, Louie Fuller. The portrait of Maria Feodorovna is flanked by pictures of two earlier Empresses – on the left, Alexandra Feodorovna, the consort of Nicholas I, and, on the right, another Maria Feodorovna, the consort of the Emperor Paul, whose name is linked with many charitable foundations.

Right: Visiting day at the Institute. Evidently whole families visited; a number of the girls' brothers are wearing uniforms of various institutions and schools, among them that of the Alexander Lyceum.

Overleaf: Pupils of the Institute playing tennis in the gardens. Wide hats of frilled muslin are worn outside. The Institute's director, Princess Yelena Alexandrovna Lieven, is seated among the spectators on the left.

Pupils dressed for dancing. They are posed in the main hall of the Institute and behind them, between two curious electric candelabra, hangs the portrait of Empress Maria Feodorovna to which pupils were required to make a daily curtsey.

Exercise class in the gymnasium of the Smolny Institute.

Pupils of another institute – that named after the Empress Maria – skating on a frozen lake.

Opposite: A pupils' lunch, celebrating the anniversary of the founding of the Imperial Alexander Lyceum, the Eton of Russia. The Lyceum was founded in 1811 by Alexander I, on the advice of the statesman Speransky, and was originally housed in a building adjoining Tsarskoye Selo, a wing of the palace. The purpose of the Lyceum was to educate the sons of the aristocracy to fit them for careers in government or the services. The course was extremely hard and the regime spartan. Pupils, admitted between the ages of ten and twelve, were enrolled in two successive courses, each running for three years without the right to return home during holidays. Parents from wealthier backgrounds were reluctant to part with their children for the requisite six years so pupils tended to be drawn from the ranks of the impoverished gentry whose children needed to be fitted for a career. Many pupils became eminent in a range of professions, primarily in government services – among them the poet Pushkin, Prince Gorchakov (see page 101) and the great navigator, Admiral Matushkin.

The boys wear blue cotton coats with silver tabs and buttons, and white trousers. At the

end of the hall is a portrait of the founder, Alexander I. The pupils eat from plain white porcelain painted with the Imperial monogram.

Count Kokovstov, a former pupil who became one of the most distinguished statesmen under Nicholas II, remembers, 'I recall a number of pleasant memories associated with the centenary of the Lyceum. Since graduating in December 1872, I never lost touch with the school, always attending its annual celebration on 19 October, a day dear to me because of the sincere friendships which always existed between its pupils. In October 1911 the Lyceum marked its centenary . . . I recall it as an event of great beauty and, at the Emperor's wish, of special note. Former pupils presented a marble bust of the sovereign, and as I was in the habit of regularly seeing the Tsar it fell to me to ask his agreement to a sitting . . . From a list of proposed sculptors he selected the young academician, Kustodiev, who had worked with Repin . . . Kustodiev was at that time little known as a sculptor but the Sovereign remarked that former pupils should not be wary of selecting him, for Repin considered Kustodiev to have a great future before him. The celebrations continued for a week in early January, with a formal dinner at the Winter Place, a performance at the Marinsky Theatre attended by the entire court, a ball at the Lyceum itself and a dinner organised at the Circle of Nobility [the club of the aristocracy], while the Emperor used every occasion to tell me how pleased he was to be among the pupils and how disappointed that the state of health of the Empress prevented her and the Grand Duchesses from taking part.'

Left: Passing out examination at the Alexander Lyceum. The examining board are seated under a portrait of the reigning Emperor.

The Corps des Pages, which produced the élite warrior caste of the Empire, was housed in a palace, above, which Rastrelli had built for Count Vorontsov, the vice chancellor of the Empress Elizabeth. This and the Stroganov Palace are the only surviving examples of town houses built by Rastrelli for the nobility.

There were strict qualifications for entrance to the Corps des Pages which included an impeccably noble family background. Children were put down for entry at birth, entering at the age of twelve or thirteen. They were given five years of general education and two years of specialisation before proceeding to a guards regiment, where priority would be given to candidates whose antecedents had served in the same unit. Therefore there was a hereditary factor in the loyalty and sentiment felt by an aspiring officer.

The photographs on the right show Nicholas Pavlovich Fomin in the sumptuous uniform of a court page, and Prince Theodore Alexandrovich Romanov, son of the Tsar's sister Xenia, in winter uniform – gold collar and cuffs and gold buttons on a black tunic, with a thin red line on the black trousers. White gloves were obligatory.

The pupils of the Corps were conscious of their privileged position and were united by an oath of 'Friendship to Death'.

Recruits to the Household Cavalry Unit, with their cornet, Count A. A. Ignatiev, who later served as military attaché to Scandinavia between 1908 and 1912, and to France between 1912 and 1914.

Vladimir Alexandrovich Sukhomlinov (1848–1926), Minister for War between 1909 and 1915, with a group of officers at the celebration of the two-hundredth anniversary of the capture of Vyborg during the Northern War of 1700–21. The date is 12 June 1910.

Above: Review of soldiers in their white-jacketed summer uniforms, marching past Nicholas II and his uncle, Grand Duke Vladimir. The regimental commander is seated on his horse in the foreground of the picture. The annual army manoeuvres were held at Krasnoe Selo, near St. Petersburg.

Below: Soldiers dressed in historical army uniforms from various periods. On the right are those uniforms introduced by Alexander III to give the army a more typically Russian look – looser breeches and a less formal jacket. The new uniforms were designed by Victor Vasnetsov. Alexander Benois regretted the loss of the glamour of the earlier period.

A group of conservatoire students photographed in 1912.

Alexander Konstantinovich Glazunov, composer, conductor and teacher, the director of the Petersburg conservatoire. He was born in the city in 1865 and spent almost all his life there. Here he is pictured, seated on the left, in his study at the conservatoire. He was the composer of scores for the ballets 'Raymonda' and '*Ruses d'Amour*', of eight symphonies and five instrumental concertos.

Opposite: A montage of portraits showing teachers at the St. Petersburg conservatoire, Russia's oldest musical academy. Founded in 1862 by the composer and conductor Anton Grigoriievich Rubinstein, it actually developed out of the music classes which were held by the city's Musical Society from 1859. Among its students were such distinguished figures in musical life as Tchaikovsky and Ippolitov-Ivanov. The teachers there included Rimsky-Korsakov.

Watching the full solar eclipse that occurred in 1912. Petersburgers shade their eyes, left, the scientists at the Pulkovo Observatory use highly powered telescopes, right, while the enthusiastic amateurs, top, have brought their own smaller versions.

Guests at the celebration for the two-hundredth anniversary of the Botanical Gardens. The church banners in the background attest that a *molebin* has been held as part of the ceremony.

Celebrations for the two-hundredth anniversary of the Botanical Gardens, founded by Peter in 1713 as a physic garden on Apothecary Island. Soon workshops for medical instruments and houses for the herbalists were built nearby, and by the 1730s herbs were collected from as far away as China and Japan. In 1735 the Director, I. Sigizbek, issued the first printed catalogue of garden plants. By 1823 the Medical Gardens had become the Imperial Botanical Gardens, with a museum, library and a large complex of hothouses. At the beginning of the twentieth century they boasted one of the world's largest plant collections, specialising in Asian flora. By the two-hundredth anniversary of 1913 the Gardens had been officially named after their founder and new buildings for herbariums and the library were designed by the architect A. I. Ditrikh as part of the celebration. In this picture, the camera is turned towards the podium where a speech is being made, but we can see the ermine-framed bust of Peter the Great on the extreme right.

Professors at the Geological and Mineralogical Museum of St. Petersburg.

Moleben to mark the laying of the foundations of the building for the Imperial Geographical Society.

Religion was an integral part of Russian life, and a service of blessing was called to mark all kinds of activities. Here a priest reads prayers, attended by two deacons and a server with a holy water basin and a brush for distributing holy water. In the background are members of the choir.

Experiments in the laboratory of the Imperial Technical Institute. The uniforms bear the cypher of Nicholas I.

Members of the Imperial Technical Society at a meeting dedicated to the seventy-fifth anniversary of photography in 1914.

Overleaf: A drawing class at the Imperial Academy of Art being taught by Leonty Benois, the architect brother of Alexander. Among his buildings in the capital are the Singers chapel (attached to the Peter Paul Cathedral), the Otto Clinic on Vasilievsky Island and an annexe of the Russian Museum of Alexander III. The class is for younger pupils of the Academy, most of whom are uniformed in traditional high-necked Russian shirts.

Pupils of the Marinsky Teachers Training Seminary in an exercise class. Named after the Dowager Empress Maria Feodorovna this, like most such institutions, offered scholarships to promising students who could not afford the fees. Education was highly regarded in Russia at this time, and of an excellent standard.

Overleaf: Architectural drawing class for women students. Examples on the walls include suspension bridges, a cross-section of a church interior and a detail of an icon screen. The pupils work on a project designing churches.

Schoolgirls of the Nicholas Orphanage Institute, named after the founder Nicholas I Pavlovich, at an *al fresco* lunch in 1913. In accordance with an Imperial ukase of 1808, orphanages ran courses to train pupils as governesses. Orphans of army officers and government officials were taken into the Institute from the age of six and taught to a high standard, leaving at the age of nineteen. In 1913 the Director of the Institute was Nadezhda Vasilievna Blatsel and its honorary trustee, Count Nikolai Fedorovich Heiden. The Institute was located in a palace which had once belonged to Count Razumovsky at number 48 on the Moika Embankment.

The Vladimir Church School. In this rather posed picture of classes out-of-doors an unlikely number of activities are taking place simultaneously to reflect the variety of subjects on the curriculum. From the left, a pupil is demonstrating copperplate writing on the blackboard, others are knitting, reading, sewing, painting and playing the harmonium.

Students of the Vladimir Church School in
painting class.

Vladimir Mikhailovich Bekhterev, a famous psychiatrist and neurologist, founder of the Psychoneurologic Institute in St. Petersburg in 1908. He was also a director of the Women's Medical Institute.

The children's clinic of the Women's Medical Institute. Children playing in the hall. The Institute, founded in 1897, was funded by voluntary donations.

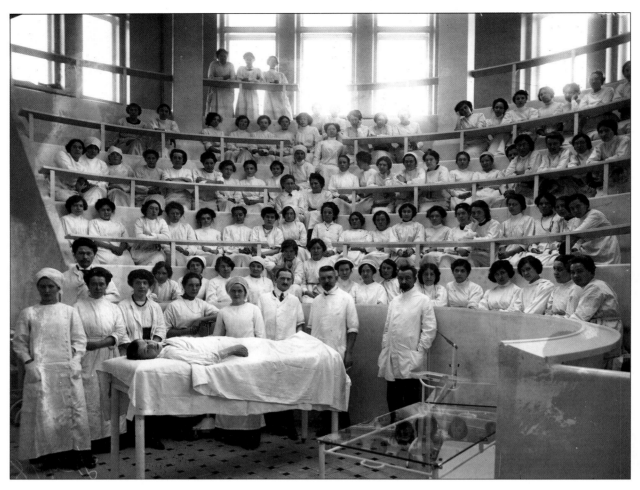

Women medical students in the theatre during a lecture. This photograph was taken by Bulla in 1913.

Instruction in first aid at the Oldenburg Institute, a women's college founded by the Grand Ducal family of Oldenburg, a branch of which had married into the Imperial house and settled in Russia.

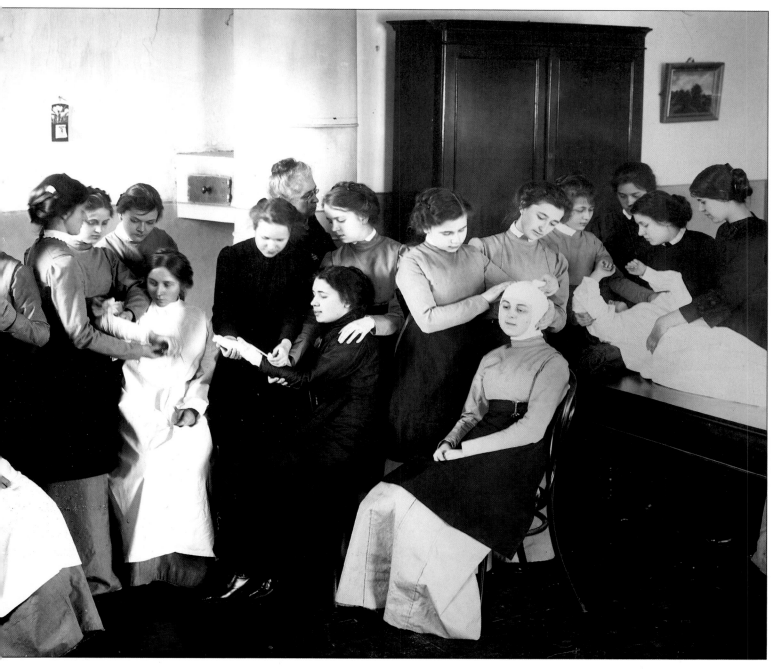

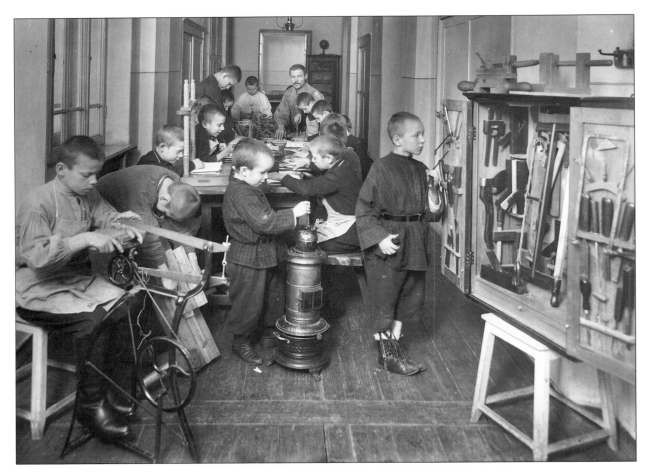

Woodwork class at a primary school. In the foreground fish glue is being heated on a small portable stove.

Children's kindergarten, probably charity-run, in the summer theatre in Petrovsky Park.

Gymnastic 'pyramids' of students. In the lower photograph, the teachers wear the cypher of one of the agricultural institutes.

A cycling champion. Cycle races were a popular sport for both participants and spectators at the turn of the century.

Contestants in a motorised tricycle race.

Members of a cyclists' society at a refreshment room in 1901.

A group of skiers. Their clothes look impractical, if not dangerous, for any form of exercise to contemporary eyes.

226

EPILOGUE

Peter's creation, his great city, was not destined to survive as an Imperial capital. The most gloomy predictions of its adversaries were justified, ironically, at a point when they seemed almost irrelevant. Throughout history the capital of all the Russias has tended to shift, depending upon where it was necessary to focus a strong political and cultural centre, from Kiev, 'Mother of Russian Cities', to Vladimir-Suzdal, then to Moscow, to St. Petersburg, then Moscow once again. Yet as a city Petersburg, although today its name commemorates not Peter but the man who degraded it from its status as a capital, remains. Its architecture, in contrast with that of Moscow, survives intact.

The photographs of this final section evoke war. There were two disastrous wars at the beginning of the century, and no doubt if Alexander III had lived they both would have been avoided. The first was sparked off by a Far Eastern adventure engineered by disreputable advisors close to the young Tsar, and against the advice of his appointed Minister for Foreign Affairs, which provoked the intervention of Japan. It was widely said that the Minister for the Interior, Plehve, held the opinion that Russia required 'a small victorious war' in order to resolve dissatisfaction with the country. The result was very different. The unsuccessful outcome of hostilities abroad provoked complications at home. The full extent of public dissatisfaction came to the surface and for the first time the brittleness of the situation was fully revealed. Political demonstrations in the capital erupted with a mass rally planned to converge on Palace Square – the tragic events of Bloody Sunday. Meanwhile in the countryside there was anarchy as the peasantry, unreconciled to the distribution of land after the emancipation of 1861, set fire to the estates.

In 1905 the Empire was brought to the verge of breakdown. Yet the government was able to regain control of the situation. The troops, who remained loyal, were successfully brought back from the Far Eastern front, favourable peace terms with Japan were achieved through the diplomatic ingenuity of Count Witte, and the economy was salvaged by a loan from Russia's French allies. At last a real attempt was made to deal with the grievances of the various alienated sections of the population – a greater autonomy for the non-Russian provinces, religious toleration for all, and a platform for the liberal intelligentsia through the institution of a parliament. Russia was not yet a constitutional state governed through elected representatives of the people, for the monarchical principle was upheld through the Tsar's remaining – and important – prerogatives: his right to appoint ministers, to determine foreign policy and to declare peace and war. But there were hopes among a section of the intelligentsia that government on the British model could be transported from the banks of the Thames to those of the Neva.

Surprisingly quickly life returned to normal. The violence that had been unleashed was frightening – a reminder of the uncharted explosive force which lay below the surface. The sheer inconvenience of anarchy made the liberals conscious of their differences with the extremists working for the upheaval of

A *molebin* held in the white-and-gold throne room of the Winter Palace to mark the inauguration of the state *Duma* (parliament) in 1906. The occasion was the first at which representatives of all classes had assembled in one room. On the left are the ministers and advisers, the military and civil functionaries and the courtiers, and on the right the newly chosen representatives of the country – the land owners, lawyers, merchants, nobles and peasants. In the foreground one can see the Icon of the Holy Visage (see page 62).

Crucial to the abortive revolution of 1905 was a mass demonstration organised by the priest, Father George Gapon, an enigmatic character whose ultimate political allegiance has never been determined. Ostensibly a loyal subject with a mission to alleviate the conditions of the working class, nevertheless it is clear that he had close ties with revolutionary agitators among the Social Democrats who produced a political programme of reforms in the shape of a petition which it was planned that leaders of the demonstration should deliver to the Winter Palace. Gapon planned the march to take place shortly after the fall of Port Arthur to the Japanese, and the demonstrators carried icons and Imperial portraits both as personal insurance and to give an impression of loyalty. The government, taken by surprise, lacked an adequate police force to disperse the gathering. At the same time it was felt that whatever reforms needed to be introduced, these could not be extracted from them by a mob – a situation analogous to that of the French Revolution when Louis XVI placed the cap of Liberation on his head prior to a complete loss of control. Troops were therefore positioned to block the approaches to Palace Square, the crowds, pushed from behind, refused to disperse, and the soldiers, after a warning volley in the air, fired at them. Estimates of the casualties of Bloody Sunday, as it came to be known, inevitably ranged from the official figure of 130 dead and the claims of the revolutionaries that over a thousand had fallen.

social revolution, and encouraged the conservatives to seek consensus among the population at large. Stolypin's radical agrarian reform – a redistribution of land to the peasantry – was, as he termed it, 'a wager on the strong', while his suppression of sedition was ruthless. Under his successor as Minister of the Interior, Kokovtsov, the Russian economy gave good results, and during this time a number of leading thinkers of the radical intelligentsia abandoned their Marxist beliefs and embraced Orthodoxy. Thus the planned economy and the spontaneous development of the country were unfavourable to further revolutionary activity.

Then came 1914, the second military conflict, at a time when the country above all needed peace and time to resolve the constitutional crisis and for the land reforms to take effect. The war, which Russia was obliged to wage

The launch of a warship built in the Admiralty dockyard in 1914.

230

through her commitments to allies, was disastrous; even in victory, it is difficult to see what positive results might have accrued. It put a terrible strain on the government, the administration and the people – a strain under which eventually everything broke down.

The collapse of 1917 remains beyond the horizon at the time these photographs were taken and is moreover too complex and too controversial to deal with in passing, particularly as, so the noted historian of the February Revolution, Katkov, reminds us 'the history of 1917 has been bedevilled by unconscious distortion and deliberate falsification'. It is enough to say that the city on the eve of breakdown was rife with rumour; the unprecedented campaign of slander being waged surprised those who returned home from the front. The most persistant of these rumours concerned an alleged pro-German

One of the many charitable organisations working for the war effort arranged for ordinary soldiers to be entertained in middle-class homes. Here, an ill-at-ease soldier is sharing a meal with an obviously wealthy family.

faction at Court and a dishonourable peace on which, it was claimed, the government was intent. In response, the liberal opposition demanded a transfer of power to an 'administration of public confidence' maintaining that the war could not be won so long as government remained autocratic. This liberal campaign prepared the psychological climate for the outbreak of the February Revolution in the streets of the capital, but nothing turned out as predicted. The removal of the Tsar did not bring victory closer. On the contrary the undermining of legitimacy led inexorably to total collapse and to the emergence of new and unforeseen developments, for the Bolshevik experiment that supplanted the Petrine Empire was both more radical and more Westernising than any blueprint of Peter's to reshape Russia's destiny.

The Emperor, accompanied by the Tsarevich, inspects a guards regiment in 1916.

Opposite above: Selling flags for the war effort.

Opposite: Members of the Women Workers' Committee for the Wounded sewing for soldiers at the front.

232

Nicholas II and Grand Duke Michael on a visit to a Red Cross hospital. The Cossack on the right of the picture is one of the Tsar's personal bodyguard.

Tending the wounded on a Red Cross hospital train.

A soldier's funeral. His widow stands in the foreground and members of his regiment stand to attention on the left as a priest bestows a blessing.

Demonstrations of patriotic fervour in Palace Square on the declaration of war in 1914.

Nicholas II on the balcony of the Winter Palace on the day that war was declared in May 1914. Vassilyev, the Chief of Police in St. Petersburg, recorded the occasion in his memoirs: 'I was myself in the midst of the frenzied throng and allowed myself to be carried along to the Winter Palace. Wherever I looked I saw nothing but joyous resolve expressed in the faces around me . . . The doors were flung open, the Tsar stepped out onto the balcony, and in the same instant the tens of thousands in the open space fell upon their knees . . . the Empress also showed herself to the crowd . . . she was covering her face with her hands and the convulsive movement of her shoulders suggested that she was weeping. The sovereigns were hailed with thunderous exaltation.' Nicholas did not share the crowd's enthusiasm. Unable to prevent war, he was nonetheless aware that it was a trial unlikely to bring anything good for Russia.

FURTHER READING

E. M. Almedingen, *The Emperor Alexander II*, London, 1962

J. F. Baddeley, *Russia in the Eighties*, London, 1921

Karl Baedeker, *Russia*, London, 1914

Maurice Baring, *Landmarks in Russian Literature*, London, 1960
The Mainsprings of Russia, 1914

André Bely, *Petersburg*, translated by R. Maguire and John Malmsted, Sussex, 1978

Alexandre Benois, *Memoirs* (two volumes), London, 1960

Meriel Buchanan, *The Dissolution of an Empire*, London, 1932

Marquis de Custine, *Russia*, London, 1854

Jacques Ferrand, *Noblesse Russe: Portraits* (volumes I and II), Paris, 1985, 1986

Kyril Fitzlyon and Tatiana Browning, *Before the Revolution*, London, 1977

John Foster Fraser, *Russia of Today*, London, 1915

Patrick de Gmelini, *La Garde Imperiale Russe*, Paris, 1986

Stephen Graham, *Russia in Division*, London, 1925
Tsar of Freedom, New Haven, 1935

Camilla Gray, *The Great Experiment; Russian Art 1862–1922*, London, 1962

Lord Frederick Hamilton, *Vanished Pomps of Yesterday*, London, 1943
Handbook for Travellers in Russia, Poland and Finland, London, 1875

George Heard Hamilton, *The Art and Architecture of Russia*, London, 1954

Augustus Hare, *Studies in Russia*, London, undated

N. Jarintzov, *The Russians and Their Language*, Oxford, 1916

Tamara Karsavina, *Theatre Street*, London, 1930

George Katkov, *Russia, 1917*, London, 1967

Laurence Kelly, *St. Petersburg: A Traveller's Companion*, London, 1981

Victor and Audrey Kennett, *The Palaces of Leningrad*, London, 1973

Countess Kleinmichel, *Memories of a Shipwrecked World*, London, 1923

Johann Kohl, *Russia: St. Petersburg, Moscow, Kharkov, Riga, Odessa, the German Provinces on the Baltic, the Steppes, the Crimea and the Interior of the Empire*, London, 1842

Count V. N. Kokovstov, *Iz Moevo Proshlavo*, Paris, 1932

Marchioness of Londonderry, *Russian Journal, 1836–7*, London, 1973

Marvin Lyons, *Russia in Original Photographs*, Boston, 1977

Sir Donald Mackenzie-Wallace, *Russia* (two volumes), London, 1903

Christopher Marsden, *Palmyra of the North*, London, 1932

A. Mossolov, *At the Court of the Last Tsar*, London, 1935

Rosa Newmarch, *The Russian Arts*, London, 1916

Henry Norman, *All the Russias*, London, 1902

Chloe Obolensky, *The Russian Empire: A Portrait in Photographs*, London, 1980

S. S. Oldenburg, *Tzarstdovanie Imperatora Nikolaya II*, Belgrade, 1939

Maurice Paléologue, *An Ambassador's Memoirs, 1914–17*, London, 1973

Princess Romanovsky-Krassinsky, *Dancing in Petersburg. The Memoirs of Kschessinska*, London, 1960

The Russian Diary of an Englishman (anonymous), London, 1919

Prince Sergei Shcherbatov, *Khudojnik v Ushudshei Rossii*, New York, 1955

Henri Troyat, *Daily Life in Russia under the Last Tsar*, London, 1961

Count P. Vassili, *Behind the Veil at the Russian Court*, London, 1913

Ian Vorres, *The Last Grand Duchess*, London, 1964

Anna Vyrubova, *Memoirs of the Russian Court*, New York, 1925

Vladimir Weidlé, *La Russie Absente et Presente*, Paris, 1949

Nadine Won-Larsky, *The Russia That I Loved*, London, undated

Prince Felix Youssupoff, *Lost Splendour*, London, 1953

INDEX

(Figures in italics refer to captions)